WELCOME

Follow Taylor Swift's rise from teen breakthrough act to global superstar in this ultimate fanbook. As one of the world's biggest stars – voted both Artist of the Decade and Woman of the Decade – Taylor Swift's career goes from strength to strength. After two critically acclaimed surprise lockdown albums, the new versions of *Fearless*, *Red* and *Speak Now*, and her record-breaking tenth album *Midnights*, it's been a busy few years for Miss Swift. But Taylor shows no sign of slowing down any time soon, as she continues the monumental Eras Tour in celebration of her entire career so far.

In this special edition, we look back on how Taylor's music and style have evolved over the years, from her self-titled country-infused debut, through the retro 80s vibe of *1989*, to the stripped-back indie of *folklore* and *evermore* and the dreamy electro-pop of *Midnights*. Discover how her relationships and personal life have shaped her songwriting and performances, and how this superstar uses her influence to support causes close to her heart.

© Johannes Eisele/AFP via Getty Images

CONTENTS

CHAPTER ONE
Becoming Miss Americana **006**

CHAPTER TWO
The Evolution of Taylor Swift **022**

CHAPTER THREE
Team Taylor **088**

CHAPTER FOUR
Style & Substance **106**

CHAPTER FIVE
Superstar **126**

CHAPTER 1

BECOMING MISS AMERICANA

© Michael Buckner/Getty Images

BECOMING MISS AMERICANA

FROM CHRISTMAS TREES TO COUNTRY HITS, DISCOVER TAYLOR SWIFT'S JOURNEY TO BREAK INTO THE BUSINESS

WORDS BY ELLA CARTER

Born on 13 December 1989 in Reading, Pennsylvania, Taylor Alison Swift came into the world destined for greatness. Her parents gave her the androgynous name Taylor (after the classic American singer-songwriter James Taylor) in the hope that it might further her chances of success. Even as a tiny newborn, a bright future was already in the works...

Taylor spent much of her childhood in Wyomissing, Pennsylvania. She lived with her parents, Scott and Andrea, and her younger brother, Austin, at the family Christmas tree farm which her father (who worked as a stockbroker) had bought from a client. "I had the most magical childhood," Swift told *Rolling Stone* in 2009 "...running free and going anywhere I wanted to in my head." The family had horses too, which Taylor rode competitively, but she, like many other little kids, was also obsessed with fairy tales, Disney songs, and then – of course, inevitably – with music.

Taylor's maternal grandmother, Marjorie Finlay, was an opera singer. The Swift family have said that Taylor shared many qualities with her, and it was Marjorie who inspired Taylor to become a singer. In a 2014 interview with *Esquire*, Taylor described her grandmother as beautiful and graceful – "she'd get up and sing, and, of course, it was the perfect, beautiful operatic voice. Gorgeous soprano."

The Swifts are a very close family. Taylor describes her mum, Andrea Swift, as her "favourite person in the world" and praises her for raising Taylor to be logical and practical in addition to shooting for the stars. Formerly a marketing executive, Andrea played a pivotal role in supporting her daughter as her career and fame snowballed, and helped to set up her daughter's MySpace page and website when Taylor's career was in its infancy. Taylor's former manager, Rick Barker, told *Entertainment Weekly* in 2008: "[Taylor's] mom and dad both have great marketing minds. I don't want to say fake it until you make it, but when you looked at her stuff, it was very professional even before she got her deal."

Taylor describes her father, Scott Swift, as "just a big teddy bear who tells me everything I do is perfect," also adding, "business-wise, he's brilliant." Yet when asked about what it's like to manage their daughter's career, the Swifts are reported to have said that it's "just like soccer practice."

Supported by her family, as a youngster Taylor took to performing early. Her mum took her on regular trips to New York to see Broadway productions and she attended musical theatre classes. But it was singing that really became her passion. By the age of 10, Swift was singing at local fairs and events. At the age of just 11 she performed 'The Star-Spangled Banner' at a Philadelphia 76ers basketball game, receiving a standing ovation at the end.

At first, Taylor and her mum Andrea would make regular trips to Nashville so that Taylor could put her work in front of the labels and producers of Nashville's Music Row. "I took my demo CDs of karaoke songs, where I sound like a chipmunk," Taylor recalled in her interview with *Entertainment Weekly*, "...and my mom waited in the car with my

Taylor rehearsing backstage at the Academy of Country Music New Artists' Show in May 2007.

A young Taylor performing the national anthem at an NFL game in 2008.

little brother while I knocked on doors up and down Music Row. I would say, 'Hi, I'm Taylor. I'm 11; I want a record deal. Call me.'"

But when the phone wasn't ringing for her demo recordings of cover songs, Taylor quickly realised that the way to make her mark would be to start writing original material.

In the same *Entertainment Weekly* interview from 2008, Andrea Swift describes the first time her 12-year-old daughter came across a 12-string guitar; "She thought it was the coolest thing." Taylor is famously stubborn and driven, and so even then this became a project to overcome and to prove that she was worthy of stardom. Her mother continued, "Of course we immediately said, 'Oh no, your fingers are too small.' Well, that was all it took. Don't ever say 'never' or 'can't do' to Taylor. She started playing it four hours a day."

Netflix's 2020 documentary, *Miss Americana*, explores Swift's journey to stardom and offers a rare glimpse into Taylor and her family's day-to-day lives. Footage of a young tween Taylor shows her performing at various events with the confidence of a seasoned pro, while other clips show her performing original songs at home on her guitar.

During one of these home video performances, a young Taylor introduces one original song by describing it as "about a girl who's just... different." She began writing songs by telling stories about her experiences and emotions, and it's a tradition that has continued throughout her expansive career. "I never felt like the kids in school were right about me when they'd say, 'She's weird. She's annoying. I don't want to hang out with her,'" Taylor explained in an interview with *Esquire* in 2014. "I always remember writing in my journal, saying, I just have to keep writing songs. I just have to keep doing this and someday, maybe, this will be different for me. I just have to keep working."

A fiercely determined kid and a self-confessed perfectionist, this mantra would indeed become a reality. Taylor's main inspiration for songwriting is rooted in country music, and her love for the genre was sparked when her parents took her to see LeAnne Rimes in concert at six years old.

From there, Taylor looked up to classic country singers such as Dolly Parton and Patsy Cline. She has said she was greatly influenced by "the great female country artists of the '90s'." Shania Twain was a huge source of inspiration, Faith Hill was her idol for everything, from music to fashion, and she admired The Chicks for their sheer attitude and their ability to play their own instruments. A whole host of other artists contributed to her melting pot of inspiration (she was and still is a huge Britney

ABOVE: Taylor's childhood home in Wyomissing, PA, where the Swift family lived before moving to Tennessee.

RIGHT: "This is definitely the highlight of my senior year!" – Taylor receiving the CMA Horizon Award in 2007.

Spears fan), but it was through country that Taylor chose to make her mark on the music industry.

"Country music teaches you to work," Taylor told *Esquire* in 2014. "I've never been more proud to have come from a community that's so rooted in songwriting, so rooted in hard work and in treating people well. It was the best kind of training."

And hard work is precisely what Taylor and her family put in. At age 13, Taylor landed a spot on an artist development program with RCS Records in Nashville, but this only lasted for a year. She decided to opt out of renewing the deal, as she was laser-focused on her dream of writing and recording her own material. "It's not a really popular thing to do in Nashville, to walk away from a major record deal," Taylor admitted in an interview with *Entertainment Weekly* in 2007, "But that's what I did, because I wanted to find some place that would really put a lot of time and care into this." She goes on, "I didn't want to just be another girl singer. I wanted there to be something that set me apart. And I knew that had to be my writing."

It was this desire to write and perform original material that led her to become the youngest person to ever sign as a songwriter with Sony/ATV Publishing at the age of 14.

Spurred on by her ultra-determined goal, it became apparent to the Swift family that Taylor's career needed more than just regular trips to the renowned Music City, where artists and record labels combine to generate the alternative nickname of 'The Songwriting Capital of the World'. Her parents were adamant that they should support their daughter in her goal of becoming a recording artist, while at the same time offering her as 'normal' a life as possible. So when Taylor was 14, the entire family made the pivotal decision to leave their home on the Christmas tree farm in Pennsylvania and made a new life in Hendersonville, Tennessee – a town about 20 minutes north of Nashville.

Once fully immersed in the Nashville music scene, Taylor began working even harder to showcase her talent. At a writers round, where songwriters get together to perform their material, she met Liz Rose – one of Nashville's songwriting heavyweights. Rose would go on to become Taylor's

13

"WHEN YOU'RE SINGING, YOU CAN HEAR THE ECHO OF PEOPLE IN THE AUDIENCE SINGING EVERY SINGLE WORD WITH YOU, AND THAT WAS THAT BIG DREAM THAT I HAD FOR MYSELF."

Taylor performing on stage in Kansas City, in 2007.

15

co-writer for her first album, and in an interview with *The Washington Post* in 2016, she described their collaborative sessions as "the easiest, funnest thing I [did] all week". Such was Taylor's flair for songwriting that Rose added, "The first time we wrote, I walked out and said, 'I don't know what I was doing there,' she really didn't need me."

Nashville life afforded Taylor many of these crucial introductions into the industry that she loved. In addition to her songwriting collaborations, she continued to make CDs and demos and sent them out to labels in order to find the right platform to launch what would turn into an exceptional, award-winning career.

One such package landed on the desk of Scott Borchetta, a record executive who at the time was working for Universal Records. Taking on *Larry King Now*, Borchetta revealed how he went to see her perform at the Bluebird Cafe. An unassuming venue set in a strip mall outside downtown Nashville, the Bluebird Cafe is a music industry institution, where the 90 seats are filled night after night with people eager to hear artists perform original work. In November 2014, a 15-year old Taylor Swift was one of these performers, and after her set Borchetta met with her and her family.

They got on well, and despite offering to provide an intro to Universal Records, Taylor put her faith in Borchetta as he set up his own label – Big Machine Records. "I felt like I needed my own direction and the kind of attention that a little label will give you," Taylor told *Entertainment Weekly* in 2007. "I wanted a record label that needed me, that absolutely was counting on me to succeed. I love that pressure." The label would go on to support her through six albums, before a huge battle over Taylor's master recording rights would eventually turn the relationship sour.

Under Big Machine, Taylor recorded her debut self-titled album, which launched on 24 October 2006. With 11 original tracks that Swift co-wrote, she released five as singles – the first of which was 'Tim McGraw'. Titled for and inspired by the songs of one of her favourite county musicians, this first single stayed true to Taylor's style of personal songwriting. She confesses that she wrote it while thinking about her feelings for a boy she was dating at the time. Of the writing process, she admitted later that "the idea for this song came to me in math class. I just started singing to myself."

RIGHT: "My mom and I have always been really close. She's always been the friend that was always there." Taylor pictured with her mother and father in 2013.

INSET: Taylor with her younger brother, Austin, in 2009.

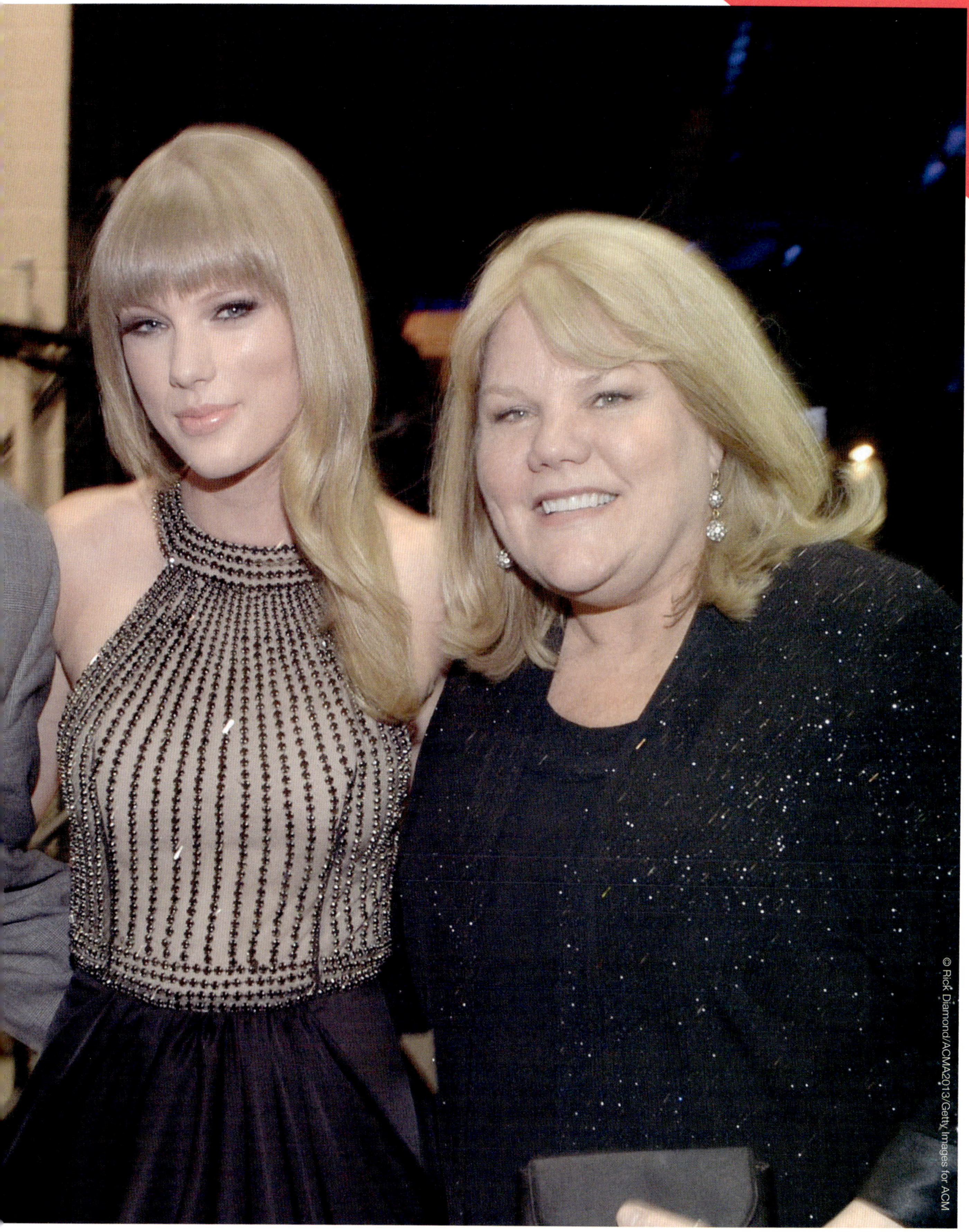

© Rick Diamond/ACMA2013/Getty Images for ACM

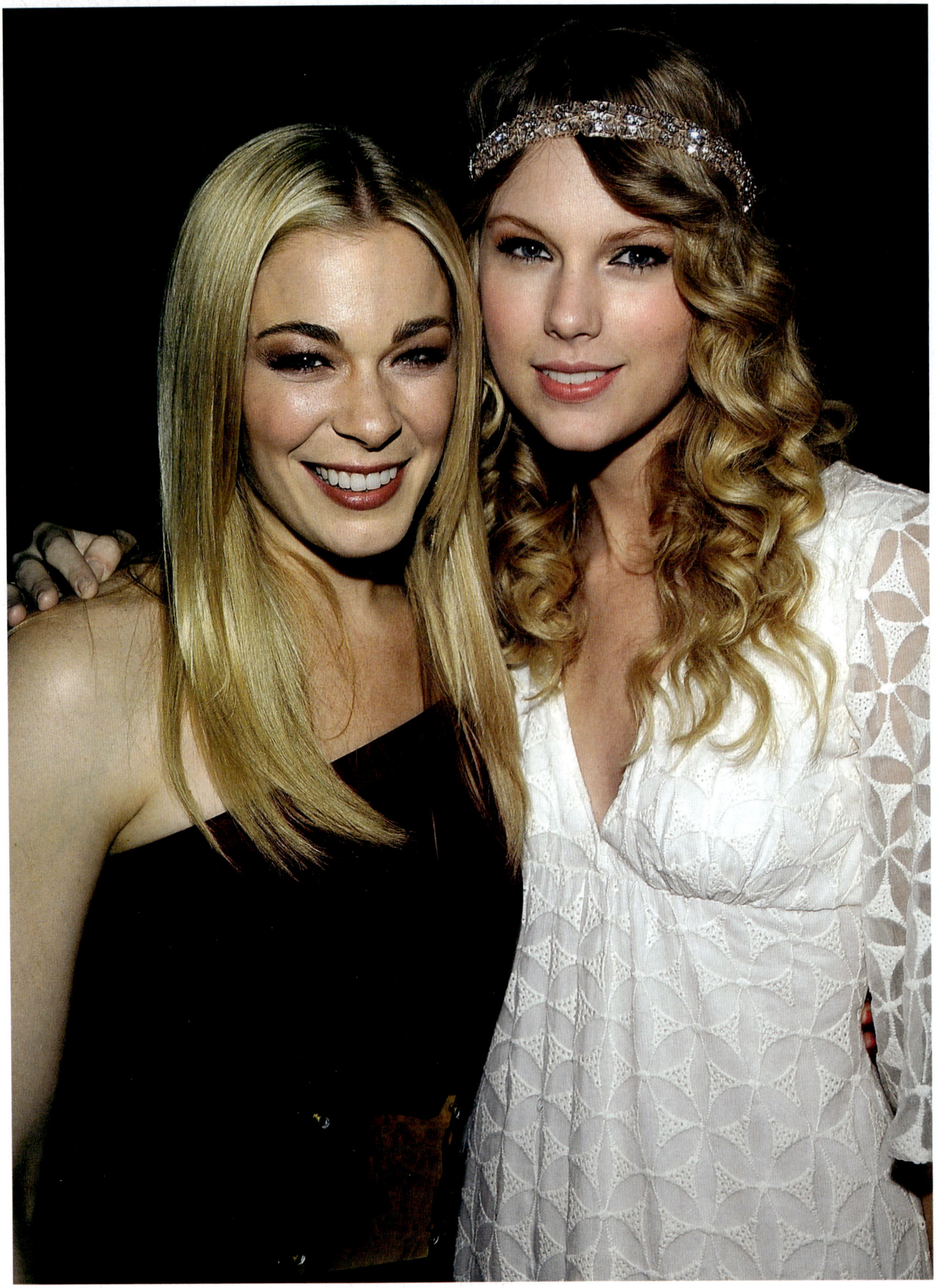

Catchy and quintessentially Taylor, 'Tim McGraw' peaked at number six on the Country Charts and reached number 33 in the Billboard Hot 100, firmly rooting Taylor Swift as a promising young artist to watch. Effortlessly bridging the gap between country music and mainstream pop, by the end of 2007 Taylor had achieved a platinum-selling album with her self-titled debut. Over 1 million copies were sold in the United States alone and she finished as the 19th best-selling album of the year and the 10th best-selling female artist of the year – all without even having finished high school. After taking home the Horizon award at the Country Music Association Awards in November 2007, Taylor famously exclaimed, "This is definitely the highlight of my senior year!"

Throughout all of this early success, Taylor was capturing fans with her down-to-earth and occasionally goofy teenage realness. With literally millions and millions of MySpace song streams, she was being herself online at a time when social media was in its infancy and she was being both accessible and relatable to her fans. "I'm just a teenager, you know?" Swift told *The Washington Post* in 2008. "I'm not going to try to act like some adult who has it all together and isn't fazed at all by that."

With the success of her debut album, Taylor began a huge touring schedule, opening the show for top country artists such as Faith Hill and Tim McGraw on their Soul2Soul II tour in 2007. Her mother accompanied her and helped her to finish high school on the road, while her dad stayed to work in Nashville. By the time she was 18, Taylor was a multi-millionaire, and yet that was just the beginning of her incredible career to come.

LEFT: Country star LeAnn Rimes was a huge influence on Taylor.

ABOVE: Taylor accepts the Breakthrough Video of the Year award for her single 'Tim McGraw' at the 2007 CMT Music Awards.

"

A LOT OF PEOPLE ASK ME, 'HOW DID YOU HAVE THE COURAGE TO WALK UP TO RECORD LABELS WHEN YOU WERE 12 OR 13 AND JUMP RIGHT INTO THE MUSIC INDUSTRY?' IT'S BECAUSE I KNEW I COULD NEVER FEEL THE KIND OF REJECTION THAT I FELT IN MIDDLE SCHOOL. BECAUSE IN THE MUSIC INDUSTRY, IF THEY'RE GONNA SAY NO TO YOU, AT LEAST THEY'RE GONNA BE POLITE ABOUT IT.

TAYLOR SWIFT

"

RIGHT: A young Taylor pictured at the FirstEnergy Stadium, in Reading, Pennsylvania, where she sang the national anthem before a baseball game on 5 April 2007.

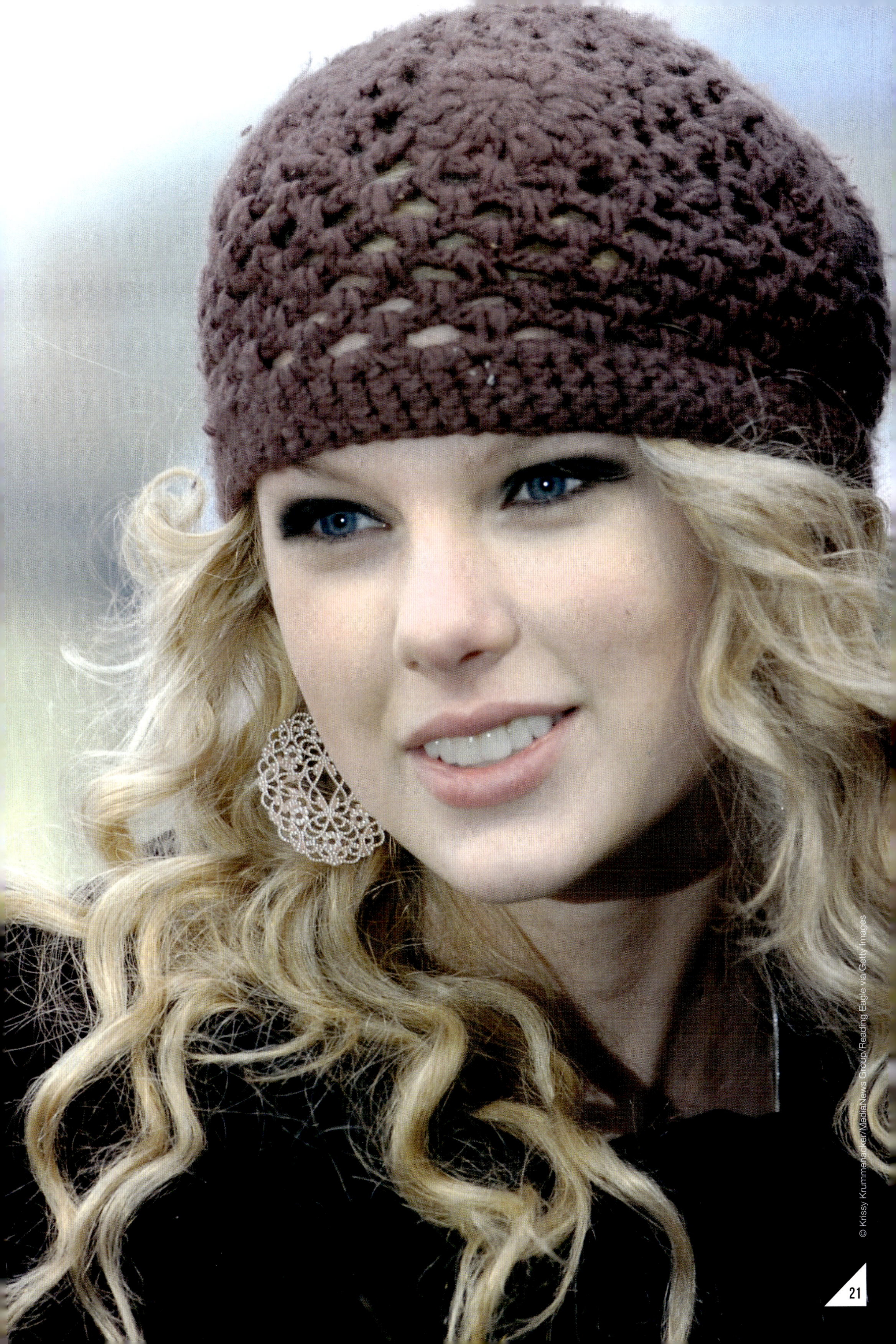

CHAPTER 2

THE EVOLUTION OF TAYLOR SWIFT

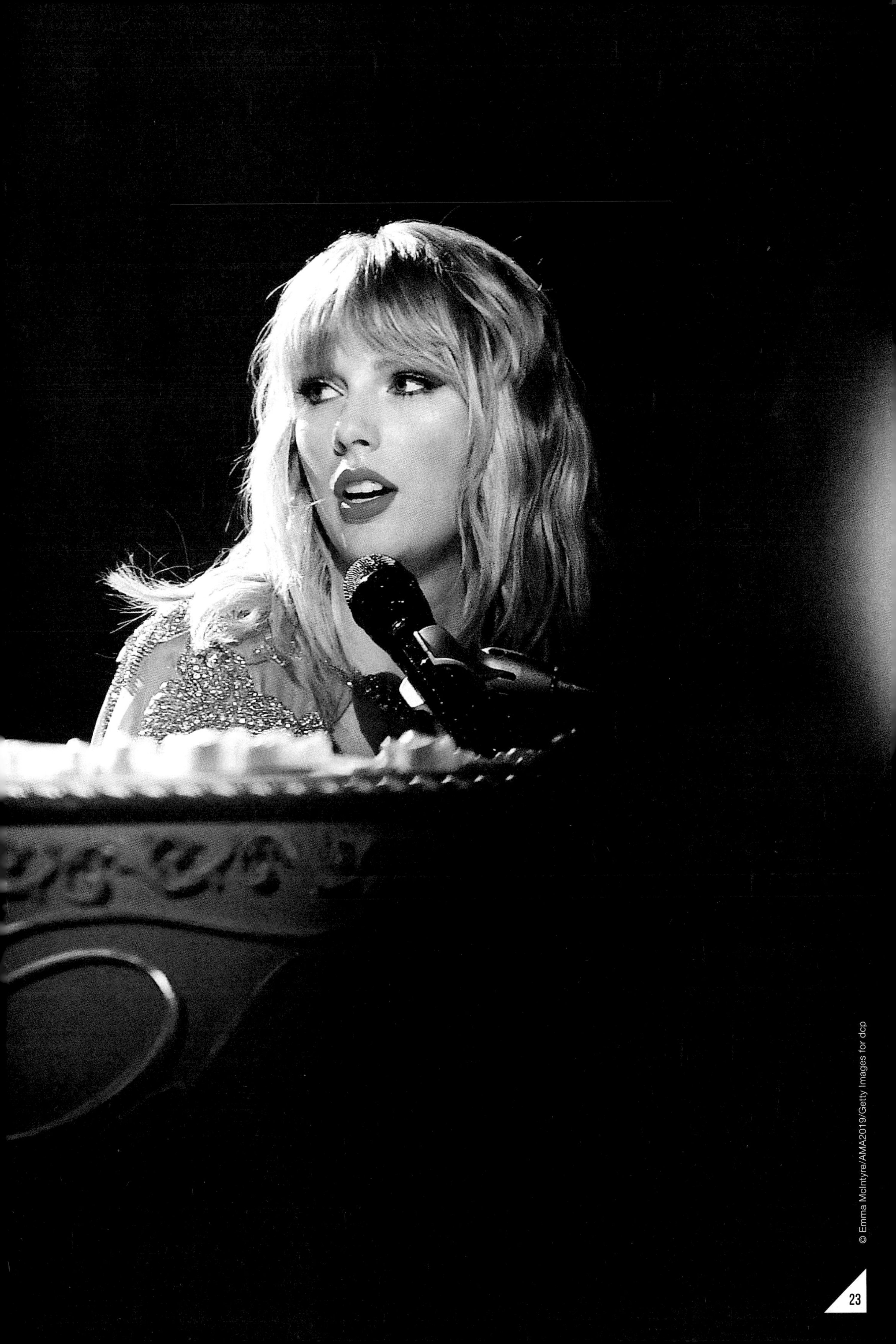

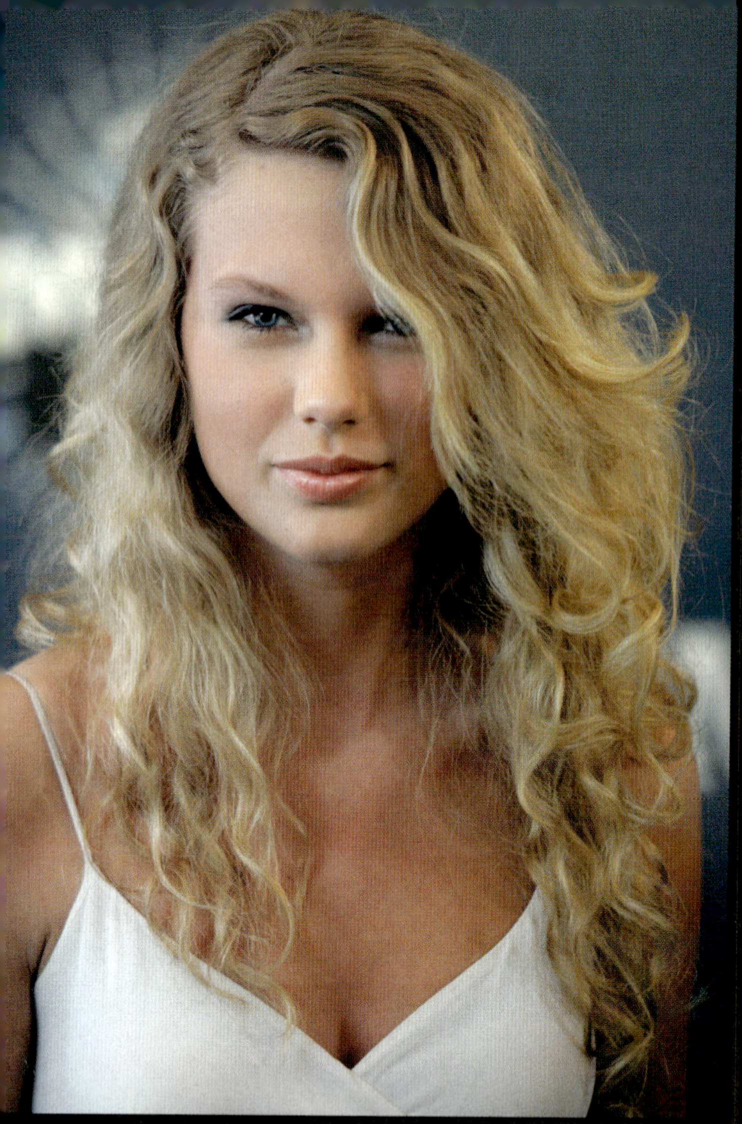

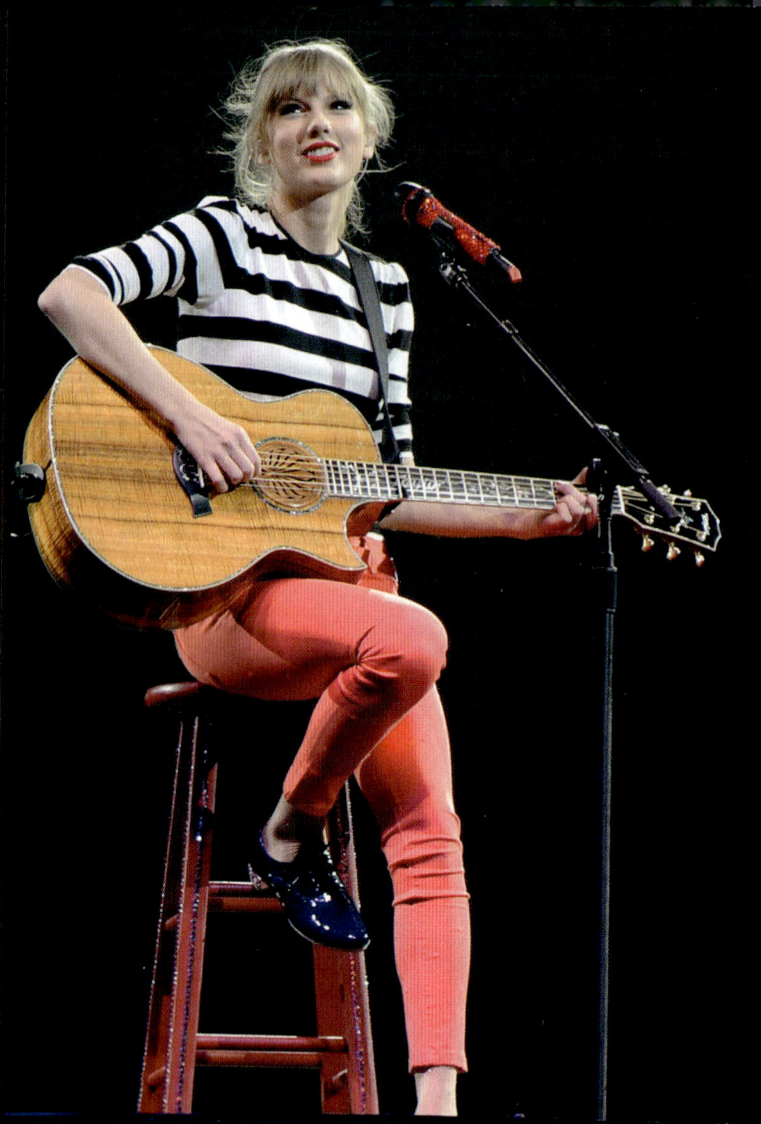

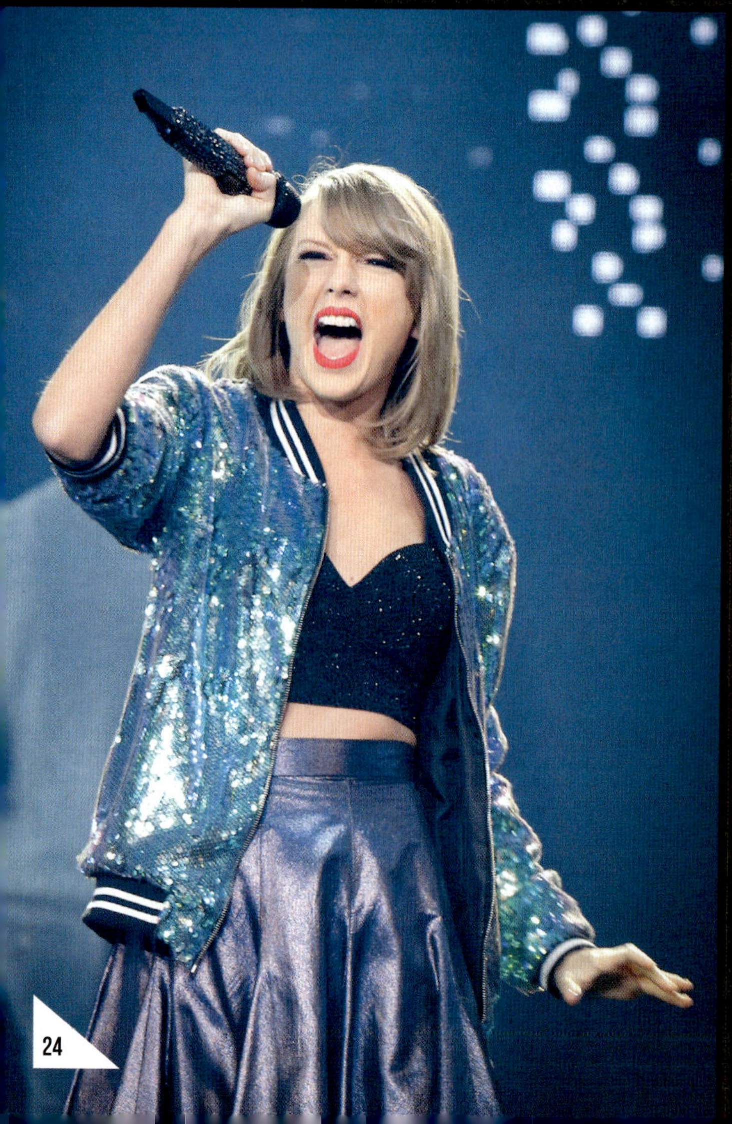

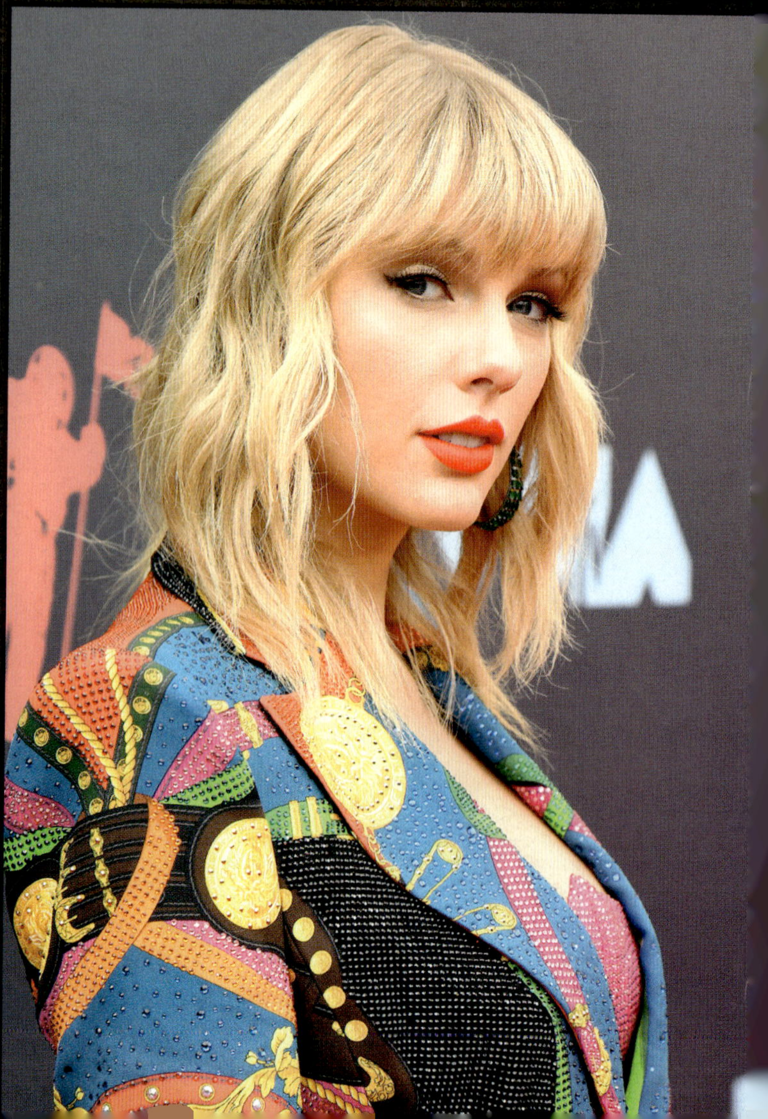

THE EVOLUTION OF TAYLOR SWIFT

THE WIDE-EYED COUNTRY STARLET TRANSFORMED INTO A REFINED RECORD-BREAKING ARTIST BY TURNING REAL LIFE INTO MARKETABLE MUSIC

WORDS BY **AMY GRISDALE**

The 16-year-old girl that took the world by storm has changed almost beyond recognition throughout her remarkable career. Now a sophisticated 30-something superstar, Taylor has evolved with every album, from her self-titled country debut, to the 80s-inspired pop of *1989*, to the reflective cinematic indie of *folklore*. While she has been something of a genre-defying chameleon over the years – incorporating elements of everything from rock and electronica, to dubstep and hip hop in her tracks – Taylor's extraordinary songwriting talent has remained at the core of her music, and has played a major role in her success.

When she was starting out in Nashville, Taylor's songwriting is what made her stand out. After the family moved from Pennsylvania to Tennessee, Taylor spent as much time writing and performing as possible. She was offered a development deal with RCA Records and had signed a songwriter contract with Sony/ATV by the time she was still only 14. The following year, Taylor signed her first record deal with Big Machine Records. She would hurry to the studio after school, often bringing high school gossip to share with her writing partner, Liz Rose. Just like the country stars that influenced Taylor as a child, she and Liz worked Taylor's real-life experiences and emotions into the catchy songs that would make up her self-titled debut album, which was released in 2006.

The lyrics throughout *Taylor Swift* displayed her maturity and unbelievable talent. She was singing about typical teenage experiences – like driving pickup trucks and sneaking out late to meet her boyfriend – but also explored the themes of monogamy, heartbreak and infidelity. It was the first impression she made on the world and established her growing brand very well. She had yet to fully form her own opinions and style but her songs were heartfelt with little flashes of comedy. She was on her way to becoming the recording artist we know and love today.

Once the album was out, Taylor's life changed dramatically. She stepped out of her ordinary life and spent most of 2006 performing, promoting her album and touring with bigger country acts to raise her profile. People loved her upbeat country sound and the honest and relatable lyrics. Critics were impressed that so many of the songs were self-written and she quickly gained notoriety for her ability to make heartfelt music that was also a commercial success. Industry professionals quickly realised that she had found an untapped market in teenagers that listened to country. Her track 'Our Song' made it to number one in the country charts and she began winning awards for both her writing and vocals.

The two years following the first album were filled with live performances, television appearances and making music videos for the singles on her first album. She was creating songs behind the scenes and learning a lot about the industry she has been launched into. By the time she was 18, Taylor's second album, *Fearless*, was ready to drop. Although her first element of pop had crept onto the album it had a very similar sound to her first record and Taylor was still very much a country artist. She continued to wear cowboy boots to her events and performances and dressed in her trademark summer dresses and flowing gowns.

Fearless started to earn her big awards. Taylor was the youngest ever recipient of a Grammy for Album of the Year at the time, and *Fearless* became one of the best-selling albums of the 21st century so far. She was already fulfilling lifelong dreams while still just a teenager. Taylor was growing up and gaining confidence; her appeal was broadening and she was learning from her experiences. At this point she was already an established celebrity, but she continued working on songs that resonated with the typical teenage experience.

Taylor released her next album two months before her 21st birthday. *Speak Now* featured a subtle shift towards more diverse musical styles and began to stray from her staple theme of romantic relationships. It was the first album she wrote completely independently without any outside help. She compiled a bank of tracks that she had written solo over the years and added some new ones that she wrote on her own late at night on tour. The music was more mature and addressed topics like losing your youth, finding your own voice and dealing with harsh media criticism. *Speak Now* featured Taylor's first apology to an ex. It reflected her growth and maturity from her early successes as a young teen. As a pop album with sprinkles of country, it appealed to a wider audience and sold more than 1 million copies in the first week.

The release of *Red* in 2012 was a significant moment in Taylor's career. The album was a blend of pop, rock and dubstep with elements of electronic and country. The themes in the lyrics were darker than her previous releases but the big hits stayed on message. 'I Knew You Were Trouble' and 'We Are Never Ever Getting Back Together' were both breakup anthems and '22' was a celebration of youth. She had made a name for herself in the industry at this point and was able to start collaborating with big names like Ed Sheeran. This was the period Taylor really switched up her look too. Gone were the sun-kissed country curls and in came the dark blonde blunt bangs. This change of image stuck and became her new trademark, including red lipstick to match her chart-topping album.

By the time *1989* was released, Taylor had completed her transition from country singer to mainstream artist. Despite her astronomical success, being on the global stage meant the entire world was free to criticise her. She responded by using her songwriting superpower. 'Shake It Off' was the first single from her fifth album and it was a response to the unprovoked unpleasantries that had been directed at her. 'Blank Space' addressed the public perception of her dating life. She was under fire in the tabloids for having – what people deemed – too many boyfriends, but releasing a song poking fun at the situation was her genius way to clap back. She had reached the point where she was confident enough to own how she was being perceived in the media and talented enough to be able to respond with a number one hit.

Taylor's high-profile feud with Kanye West reared its ugly head in 2016. After Taylor objected to being insulted in his song 'Famous', Kayne and his wife Kim Kardashian released a recording that appeared to feature Taylor giving the track her blessing. The clip had been edited and there's a chance it may have been manipulated to direct blame towards Taylor. Regardless, she received a barrage of backlash and withdrew from public appearances for a year. She spoke about the experience of feeling hated by the whole planet in the 2020 documentary *Miss Americana*. Throughout her time behind closed doors she evaluated what was truly important to her and started writing songs about what was in her heart. She stepped back into the spotlight with a new album called *reputation*. Her public image had taken a hit but she wasn't beaten by it. She used a major setback as an opportunity to shine light on the issue of artists facing unrelenting hate and feeling pressure to constantly reinvent themselves or be forgotten. She made it clear that,

FAR LEFT: Taylor's early successes saw her performing the National Anthem at sports events across the country.

LEFT: The country-pop crossover *Fearless* saw Taylor's career really take off both critically and commercially.

RIGHT: When *Speak Now* was released, Taylor was one of the biggest stars in music, and still only 20 years old.

"TAYLOR WAS FULFILLING LIFELONG DREAMS WHILE SHE WAS STILL JUST A TEENAGER."

despite Kanye West taking credit, she had earned her fame herself. She had worked incredibly hard to pursue music from being a young child and wanted the world to see she wasn't a woman that could be swept under the rug.

The driving force behind bringing big problems to the world's attention was the sexual assault she has been a victim of several years previously. In 2013 Radio DJ David Mueller groped her after reaching up her skirt during a photo op. The case came to the public attention in 2015 when the perpetrator of the assault filed defamation charges against Taylor for speaking up about it. She filed a countersuit and gave evidence in court. When the verdict ruled in favour of Taylor her attacker lost both the case and his job. The ordeal highlighted that the majority of sexual assaults on women don't get reported and many that do aren't taken seriously. It was after this event that she realised she had no choice but to use her platform to comment on world events and speak up for people that were being oppressed.

Before the release of her seventh album Taylor had yet another obstacle to face. The majority of record deals require an artist to sign over all rights to their music. Taylor was no exception and is not legally the owner of her first six albums. When it came time to renew her contract with Big Machine Records she reportedly offered to pay for ownership during negotiations. The CEO, Scott Borchetta, refused because retaining the rights to her music made the company so valuable that he could sell it for a tidy profit. Accounts vary but he offered her the chance to earn ownership by handing over even more music for the company's portfolio or remain in her contract for a further ten years. Taylor walked away from the deal and signed with a different label called Republic Records with the condition that she would retain the rights to her work. *Lover*, released in August 2019, is the first album she released that she owns outright. She wrote openly about the ordeal online to raise awareness of the issue of young artists being exploited for money.

Taylor's crusade to tackle big issues in song continued on *Lover*. Three singles were released before the album came out. The first was 'ME!' and it advocated for self-confidence and individuality. Taylor wanted her young fans to sing along and belt out the lyrics to inspire them to love themselves for who they are. 'You Need to Calm Down' came two months later. It was Taylor's first act of political expression by featuring heavy support for the LGBTQ+ community and harsh criticism for those that oppose and attempt to suppress queer culture. Even though she was sternly advised that she might suffer a dramatic economic hit for voicing

ABOVE: *Red* saw Taylor embrace other musical styles, branching out further from her country roots.

RIGHT: Taylor's fashion has evolved alongside her music. *1989* was inspired by 80s pop, and Taylor's style followed suit.

BELOW: While she has experimented with different genres over the years, Taylor's distinctive songwriting hasn't changed.

"TAYLOR WENT FROM BEING TEASED, ALONE AND UNKNOWN TO A GLOBAL SUPERSTAR."

her opinion, she felt she could stay silent on the matter no longer. The 2020 Senate primary election in her hometown of Tennessee was the inspiration for the track. In *Miss Americana* Taylor stated that the Republican candidate, Marsha Blackburn, was in favour of discrimination of gay people, opposed equal pay for women and didn't support legislation preventing violence against women while promoting herself on a platform of Christian values. Taylor felt strongly that hate is not a Christian value and urged viewers of the music video to vote for a better candidate. The third single from *Lover* was about the double-standards that women face every day of their lives. 'The Man' emphasised how the actions of women are scrutinised and interpreted differently than those of men, especially with regard to their romantic attachments. She felt that men that participate heavily in the dating world are met with praise from their peers, while women are shamed for doing the same.

Taylor's Lover Fest world tour and her Glastonbury debut were postponed due to the Covid-19 outbreak. However, she released two albums in 2020 – *folklore* and *evermore* – which she wrote and recorded during lockdown. She worked remotely with her long-time collaborator, Jack Antonoff, and The National's Aaron Dessner on both albums, leaving behind the upbeat pop of *Lover* to embrace a stripped back, indie sound. Taylor also experimented with her songwriting style, creating wistful stories around a cast of fictional characters, rather than the more personal songs that fans had come to expect.

The records were a complete surprise to both fans and critics, and not only because Taylor announced their existence mere hours before each release. The low-fi sound and Taylor's evolved songwriting style were quite different to any of her previous albums, but many music journalists regard them as the best albums of her career so far.

Not long after *folklore* and *evermore*, Taylor also began her re-recording project to regain ownership of her first six albums. The first two of these symbolic *Taylor's Versions* – *Fearless* and *Red* – were released in 2021 and both were hugely successful. The new editions included songs "From the Vault", which were tracks that didn't make the original cut of each album. On *Red (Taylor's Version)*, this included the epic 'All Too Well (10 Minute Version)', which broke the record for longest number-one song in chart history.

In October 2022, Taylor returned to pop with her tenth studio album *Midnights*, but this was not the same flavour of pop as *1989* or *Lover*. A concept album inspired by her "sleepless nights", *Midnights* explored Taylor's anxieties and insecurities with confessional lyrics set to dreamy, electro-pop beats. It became the best-selling record of 2022, and critics praised the album's (sometimes brutal) honesty and self-reflection.

It was arguably her most mature album to date, with moments of darkness such as lead single 'Anti-Hero', which Taylor described as "a real guided tour throughout all of the things I tend to hate about myself". It's also one of her favourite songs she's ever written "because I think it's really honest".

Taylor has come a long way from a kid obsessed with singing to a respected musician willing to risk her reputation to do what she believes is right. She went from being teased, alone and unknown to a global superstar with fans on every continent. Even though she's been singing and writing for more than 15 years, she isn't stopping any time soon and will continue to inspire people for years to come.

Taylor performing at the iHeartRadio Z100 Jingle Ball in New York City, December 2019.

31

TAYLOR SWIFT

RELEASED: 2006   WORDS BY: AMY GRISDALE

RELEASED WHEN SHE WAS JUST 16, TAYLOR WROTE MANY OF THE SONGS FOR HER DEBUT ALBUM WHILE IN HER FIRST YEAR OF HIGH SCHOOL

TIM MCGRAW
The idea for this song came to Taylor when she was in maths class in her freshman year of high school. Her senior boyfriend was due to graduate and move away to college at the end of the school year. Writing this track helped her deal with her sadness. She wanted to capture the bittersweet nature of a painful breakup and the happy memories that go on long after the relationship is over. The title 'Tim McGraw' is about Taylor's love of the country icon and how his music will always remind her of her first high school romance. Taylor took her concept to country music writer Liz Rose and the pair finished the song in 20 minutes.

PICTURE TO BURN
Taylor herself described the second track on her album as brutally honest. It was about a high school fling that was never 'official'. Taylor was frustrated about his arrogance and selfishness. She ranted about him, shouting "I hate his stupid truck that he doesn't let me drive! He's such a redneck!" This outburst became the building blocks for the chorus and gave the song its comical edge. 'Picture to Burn' was released as a single after it got big reactions from crowds when Taylor was on tour supporting Rascal Flatts.

TEARDROPS ON MY GUITAR
This song was inspired by Taylor's unrequited feelings for a boy at school named Drew. He only saw her as a friend, but they sat together in classes and became very close. Soon he began to open up about another girl he liked and Taylor nodded along and supported him while her heart was breaking. She endured the torture of watching the pair date for several years and never told him how she felt. When the song was released he tried to make contact with Taylor but she felt too awkward to respond to any of his messages.

Taylor's debut album saw her nominated for the Best New Artist at the 50th Grammy Awards in 2007.

Taylor pictured at the 42nd Annual Academy Of Country Music Awards with two of her icons, Faith Hill and Tim McGraw (who she named her debut single after).

"I LOVE EVERYONE WHO'S INSPIRED ME TO WRITE A SONG, WHETHER YOU KNOW IT OR NOT."

A PLACE IN THIS WORLD
Not all of Taylor's songs are about love. She wrote this at 13 when she had just moved to Nashville to pursue country music. She had forgotten she had written it but found it when putting the album together three years later. She decided to include it because it was about finding her place in the world as a musical artist, and this album was the first step towards achieving her dreams. She liked it so much that she wanted to name the album after this song, but eventually went with her own name to help her get recognition.

COLD AS YOU
This is Taylor's favourite song on this entire album. She was interested in a boy who wasn't emotionally available and had had about enough. The song is about the moment she realised he wasn't who she had thought. She regretted making excuses for him and realised she was wasting her time with him. She was very pleased with the honest and vulnerable nature of lyrics that her and writing partner Liz Rose put together. This began Taylor's tradition of putting her most emotionally raw songs as the fifth track on each of her albums.

THE OUTSIDE
Taylor wrote this ballad about loneliness when she was only 12. She felt like an outcast at school and used music as an escape. She was taller than all the other girls and was obsessed with country music while everyone else was going to parties and sleepovers. She would wake up in the morning not knowing if anybody at school would talk to her or if she was about to face another day of isolation. Looking back on this period of her life, Taylor says she's thankful she wasn't one of the 'cool kids' or she might never have found music.

TIED TOGETHER WITH A SMILE
Despite still being relatively young, Taylor found she could observe other people going through struggles and produce incredible music based on what she saw. This particular track is about one of her friends who was popular in high school and performed in beauty pageants. All the girls at school were jealous and all the boys were interested in her. While she seemed to have a perfect life, this girl developed an eating disorder. Taylor wrote this song the day she found out about her friend's condition, having been struck by how easy it is to hide such deep pain behind a smile.

STAY BEAUTIFUL
Other country artists look up to Taylor Swift for having the guts to name real people in her music. Stay Beautiful is about a boy called Cory who Taylor had a thing for, but the two never got together. She has stated emphatically that a lot of her romantic songs are based on observation rather than her personal experience. She says she barely even spoke to him but was inspired to write a song just from watching him. Cory moved away before anything could happen between them and she sang this song at the school talent show after he was gone.

SHOULD'VE SAID NO
The fifth and final single of this album went platinum and topped the country charts. It's about being cheated on in a relationship where everything else was going so well. This exact thing happened to Taylor when she was 16, and the title of the track popped into her head immediately after she discovered the news. The chorus was finished in five minutes flat and she used some of what she actually said to her boyfriend as they broke up in real life. Taylor performed 'Should've Said No' at the 2008 Academy of Country Music Awards. She wore a little black dress revealed by tearaway clothes and finished the performance under an indoor waterfall.

MARY'S SONG (OH MY MY MY)
In a world full of tabloid reports of high-profile breakups and infidelity, Taylor decided to take inspiration from the elderly couple that lived next door to her family. The pair had met as children and fell in love as they grew up. They had been married a long time and Taylor was struck by how all she needed to see a good example of 'forever love' was to go home. The song she wrote in response is about how sometimes love can be everlasting even if others don't believe it.

OUR SONG
As a resourceful young girl, when Taylor didn't have 'a song' with her high school boyfriend she wrote one herself. Like 'Tim McGraw', it took her 20 minutes to write the track. She performed it in the freshman talent show in high school and her classmates and could recite large chunks after only hearing it once. 'Our Song' was received very well when she released it as a record and she began getting nominated for country music awards for it. It was hard for them to believe a girl so young could use mature themes and tell such a compelling story.

LEFT: Taylor attending the 41st Academy of Country Music Awards in 2006.

RIGHT: Taylor performing in Kansas City during the summer of 2007.

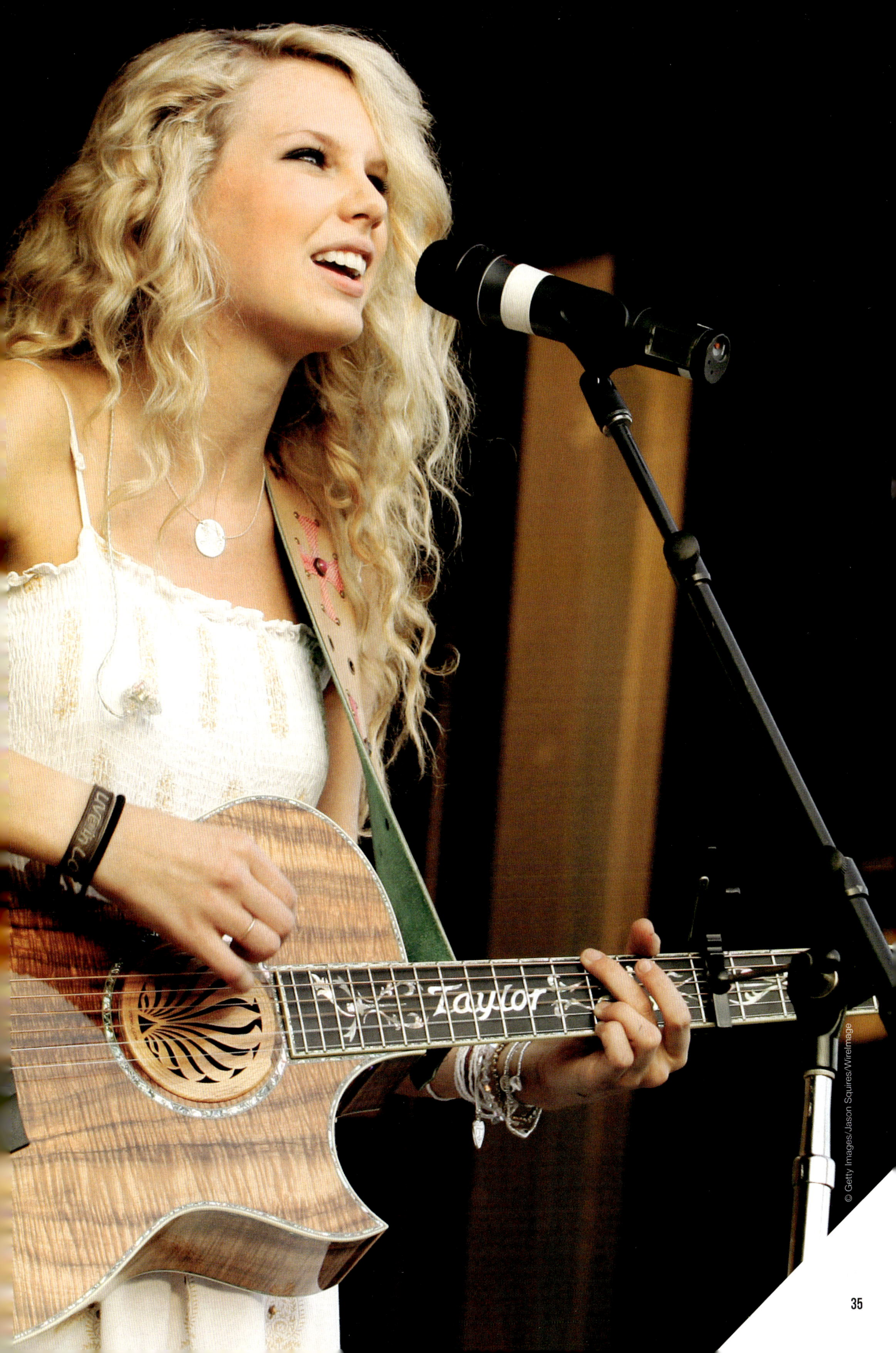
Taylor

FEARLESS

RELEASED: **2008**   WORDS BY: **AMY GRISDALE**

AFTER CREATING THIS SEAMLESS BLEND OF COUNTRY AND POP, TAYLOR BECOME THE YOUNGEST WINNER OF AN ALBUM OF THE YEAR GRAMMY

FEARLESS

By the time Taylor started writing this album she was busy touring and opening for other musical acts. She wasn't remotely close to getting into another relationship but wanted to write about the fearlessness of falling in love, regardless of the prospect of getting hurt once again. In the album's liner notes, Tyalor explains that her personal definition of 'fearless' isn't about being invincible. It's about acknowledging your fears but taking the risk anyway. She was so in love with the concept that she named her album after it.

FIFTEEN

The subject of this song is Taylor's best friend, Abigail Anderson. The song tells the story of their first year in high school together, which is the year Taylor really started to notice that she was growing up. She wanted to pen a cautionary tale including all the things she wished she'd known when she was that age. She and Abigail both had their hearts broken during freshman year. Taylor cried when recording the track because the pain of her close friends resonates deeply with her. The song makes her emotional to this day.

LOVE STORY

Influenced by *Romeo and Juliet*, this track tells the story of a forbidden romance, but thankfully the song has a much happier ending than Shakespeare's tragic play. She wrote the track on the floor of her bedroom, not wanting to stop because she felt so inspired. This was Taylor's first global hit, becoming one of the best-selling singles of all time. Critics gushed about the passionate and heart-warming nature of the song, as well as the catchy tune that fans couldn't resist singing along to.

HEY STEPHEN

A nice young man who opened a few shows for Taylor caught her eye. She was too shy to say something so she put it in a song instead. The lyrics talk about Taylor imagining the pair in romantic scenarios and wishing he would take notice of her, even though she knows it probably won't go anywhere. She reportedly sent him a text message once the album had released to tell him to check out track four. His reply was long and he was excited, but they never got together.

WHITE HORSE

Taylor wrote this track about what she says was the worst part of a break-up with someone she thought was her Prince Charming. It's that moment she realised that all of the dreams and future plans she had for the relationship were gone forever in an instant. She thought the track was a little too solemn for Fearless and planned to save it for her third album, until she was given an offer she couldn't refuse. The producers of one of her favourite TV shows, *Grey's Anatomy*, heard the song and asked to use it in the series. 'White Horse' went on to feature in the first episode of the fifth season and made it onto her second album.

ABOVE: Taylor on the red carpet at the 2008 CMT Music Awards.

FAR LEFT: Taylor performing at the Verizon Wireless Amphitheater in San Antonio, Texas, in 2008.

LEFT: Taylor attending the 57th Grammy Awards with her best friend, Abigail Anderson.

"YOU HAVE TO BELIEVE IN LOVE ... THAT'S WHY I WRITE THESE SONGS. BECAUSE I THINK LOVE IS FEARLESS."

YOU BELONG WITH ME
Taylor had the idea for this one when she overheard one of her male friends trying to soothe his angry girlfriend over the phone. She felt sorry for him and came up with the idea of a girl-next-door character that the love interest always overlooks. She plays both girls in the video alongside actor Lucas Till who appeared in the *Hannah Montana Movie* with Taylor Swift the same year. The video raked in millions of views and won the Best Female Video VMA in 2009. Her victory was overshadowed by media coverage after Kanye West stormed the stage to say that he thought Beyoncé should have won the award instead.

BREATHE
Co-written with singer-songwriter Colbie Caillat, 'Breathe' is about the ending of a friendship. Taylor and Colbie decided to keep the lyrics open to interpretation so that more fans could identify with the song. It was nominated for a Grammy for Best Pop Collaboration, but the award went to 'Lucky' by Jason Mraz and – coincidentally – Colbie Caillat. Initially Colbie was supposed to sing backing vocals on 'Breathe' but Taylor was so impressed with her work that she included much more than planned throughout the song. Taylor wanted to make sure Colbie was featured enough that fans could recognise her voice immediately.

TELL ME WHY
The day this song was composed Taylor went to the house of her writing partner Liz Rose and ranted about her relationship. Together they worked her rambling speech into a song about a girl getting sick and tired of her boyfriend hurting her feelings. It paints a picture of a boyfriend with a bad temper that constantly blows hot and cold. The man in question was not named in the song but fans speculate that it was about singer Joe Jonas. He and Taylor were together for a brief period in 2008 and unfortunately the relationship ended sourly.

FAR LEFT: Taylor with fellow singer-songwriter Colbie Caillat backstage at the 2008 AMAs.

LEFT: *Fearless* earned Taylor a clutch of awards at the 52nd Grammy Awards in 2010, including Album Of The Year, Best Country Album, Best Female Country Vocal Performance ('White Horse'), and Best Country Song ('Fearless').

YOU'RE NOT SORRY

Taylor writes music as an emotional outlet. She created this track when she had reached what she described as 'breaking point' after she had found out about a number of troubling secrets about her boyfriend. This series of discoveries was alarming enough to prompt the end of the relationship as Taylor didn't want to let him hurt her any longer. The remixed single was re-released in March 2009 on the same day Taylor had a cameo role in the 16th episode of *CSI: Crime Scene Investigation* season nine.

THE WAY I LOVED YOU

There are a lot of things that can go wrong in a relationship, especially when the couple is young and uncertain about the future. This song is inspired by the time Taylor realised that the relationship she was in was 'too perfect' and she wanted something more. She missed being so in love that it made her crazy and described the feeling as a rollercoaster rush. The lyrics talk about how they can never go back to how things used to be after this epiphany, and sometimes two people just aren't right for each other even though they may seem very compatible on paper.

FOREVER & ALWAYS

Though his name wasn't included it's widely accepted that this song is about Joe Jonas. Taylor was a guest on *Ellen* in November 2008 and told the host that 'Forever & Always' was a last-minute addition to the album. She had been through a hard break-up that occurred during a 25 second phone call. The song talks about the feeling of being under the same storm cloud when they were together and when she was alone. In another appearance of *Ellen* ten years later Taylor apologised to Joe for the savage lyrics and putting him on public blast and the pair are now friends.

THE BEST DAY

This song was a Christmas present to her mother Andrea Swift. They are extremely close and Andrea usually tours the world with her daughter. Taylor wrote this track when they were on the road and recorded it in secret. She then made a compilation of home videos, which went on to become the official music video. She played it on Christmas day and Andrea burst into tears when she realised Taylor had arranged her such a touching surprise. The song had to be dropped from the Fearless Tour set list because it made Andrea break down in tears.

CHANGE

Taylor wrote this the morning after winning a Country Music Horizon Award in 2009. She was part of a small record label in an industry full of fierce competition. She was gaining popularity and recognition even though she was still in high school. Change is about a turning of the tide towards victory from what seemed like inevitable defeat. Her songs usually contain hidden details and messages for her fervent fans. The secret meaning of this song is Taylor's gratitude that the fans were what made things change for her.

> **TO ME, 'FEARLESS' IS NOT THE ABSENCE OF FEAR. IT'S NOT BEING COMPLETELY UNAFRAID. TO ME, FEARLESS IS HAVING FEARS. FEARLESS IS HAVING DOUBTS. LOTS OF THEM. TO ME, FEARLESS IS LIVING IN SPITE OF THOSE THINGS THAT SCARE YOU TO DEATH.**
>
> TAYLOR SWIFT, IN THE FEARLESS ALBUM NOTES

RIGHT: Taylor performing at New York City's Madison Square Garden during the Fearless Tour, 27 August 2009.

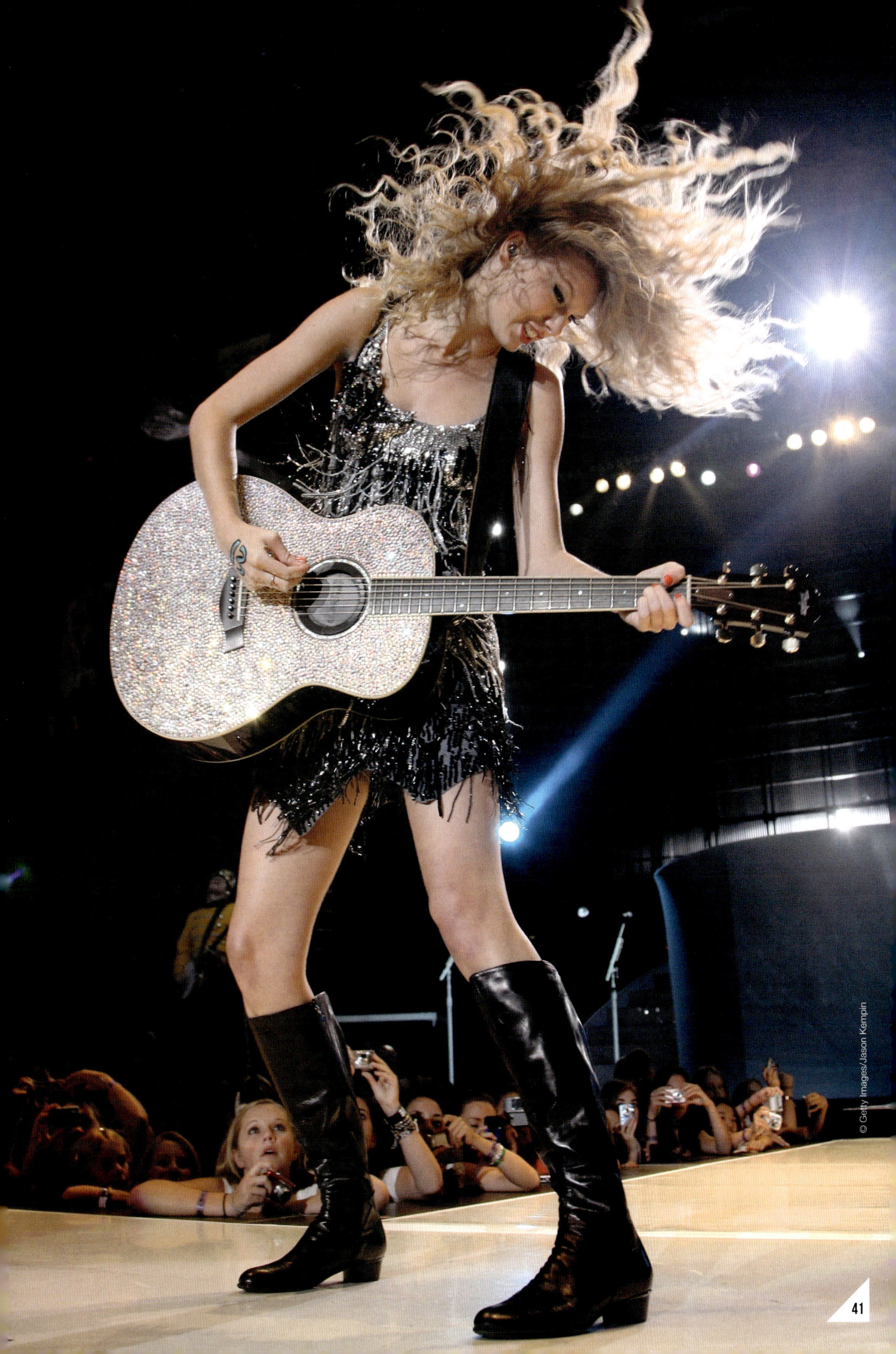

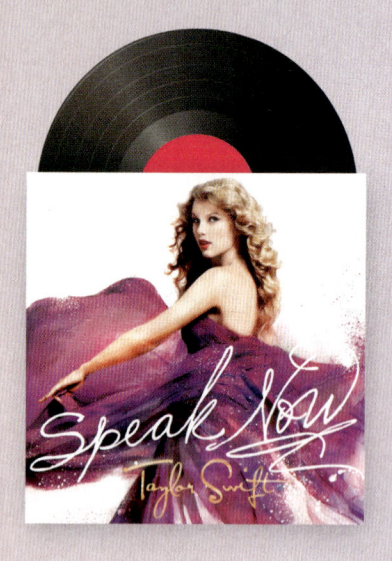

SPEAK NOW

RELEASED: 2010   WORDS BY: AMY GRISDALE

EVERY SINGLE RELEASED FROM THIS RECORD WENT EITHER PLATINUM OR MULTI-PLATINUM AND TAYLOR WROTE THE ENTIRE ALBUM SINGLE-HANDEDLY

MINE
An internet leak meant fans got to listen to this single two weeks early, forcing it to be sent out to radio stations ahead of schedule. It was the first track released from Taylor's highly-anticipated album and while it 'only' reached number two in the charts it won four of the 12 awards it was nominated for. Taylor knew the song would be a hit after recording a demo with producer Nathan Chapman in one day. The pair had a moment where they both overcome with the feeling that 'Mine' was the song to lead the charge.

SPARKS FLY
This was written back when Taylor was 16 before her first single had even come out. She performed it live in a California casino in 2007. It was played on the banjo accompanied by violins and had slightly different lyrics to the track that became part of the album. Videos of the show were put online and fans started to request she put the song out officially. Taylor was happy to oblige. She had been working on the song for years and she enjoyed seeing it change and improve to the point where it was ready to be heard around the world.

BACK TO DECEMBER
Taylor has said that this was the first time she had apologised in a song. It has never been confirmed but fans assume it is about her ex-boyfriend *Twilight* actor Taylor Lautner. They were both cast in the 2010 rom-com *Valentine's Day* and were seen together at hockey games for several months after filming had wrapped in 2009. They broke up in December that year, a month before the film came out in cinemas. The song is a message to a sweet and respectful boy expressing gratitude for the relationship and sincere regret that she couldn't fully reciprocate his feelings.

SPEAK NOW
Before a marriage takes place the officiant asks if anybody present knows of any reason why the wedding shouldn't go ahead. The congregation are told to "Speak now or forever hold your peace". Taylor had the idea for this track when she was listening to a friend complaining that her ex-boyfriend was about to marry a 'mean' girl. Taylor asked her out of the blue, "So, you gonna speak now?" and joked about storming the wedding with her guitar. She reflected later about how hurtful it must be to watch somebody you love marry somebody else and wrote 'Speak Now'.

RIGHT: Taylor performing at Madison Square Garden in 2011 as part of the Speak Now World Tour. In 2011, the tour played over 98 shows in 17 countries spanning three continents.

BELOW: The Speak Now World Tour's stage design embraced some of the 'fairy tale' elements in Taylor's songs and music videos.

43

DEAR JOHN

A Dear John letter is a term for a message written to a lover stating you no longer have feelings for them. The subject of this song is suspected to be singer-songwriter John Mayer, who Taylor dated for a few months after the pair recorded the duet, 'Half of My Heart' together. The song explores her frustrations with the relationship: "You are an expert at sorry and keeping lines blurry [...] Don't you think I was too young to be messed with?" Mayer dismissed it as 'cheap' songwriting. In response, Taylor said in an interview with *Glamour* that it was 'presumptuous' of Mayer to assume the song was about him.

MEAN

It's rumoured that this was written about blogger Bob Lefsetz who wrote scathing reviews of Taylor's music and live performances. He also had highly-publicised feuds with Kid Rock and Kiss co-founder Gene Simmons. Taylor wanted to point out that there's a difference between giving an artist constructive criticism and being downright mean. She felt that certain people were crossing the line repeatedly and attacking everything she did. Writing this song helped Taylor deal with the fact that no matter where you go in life some people are going to be mean to you.

THE STORY OF US

Running into an ex can be awkward, especially if you get seated a few feet away from each other at the CMT Awards. This is exactly what happened to Taylor Swift and John Mayer. She described it as a silent war where each was trying to show that they didn't care the other one was there. She was ignoring him and talking to people she didn't even know even though there was a person she had a lot to say to six chairs away. It made her feel like she was alone in a crowded room, and constructed a song around the frustration she felt in a situation she called "terribly, heartbreakingly awkward".

NEVER GROW UP

Taylor had mixed feelings about growing up which isn't surprising as she did it under the scrutiny of the public eye. As a child she had longed to be older and looking back she realised she should have enjoyed being a little kid as long as she could. She wrote this song as a message to her young fans. She saw herself in the faces in the crowds at her performances and wanted to tell them not to wish their childhoods away. In 2015, she dedicated a performance of the track to her godson, Leo Thames (son of model Jaime King), explaining that his birth had given the song a whole new meaning to her.

ENCHANTED
Once again Taylor was able to channel her emotional intelligence maturity into music. She met Adam Young of Owl City in New York after exchanging some phone calls and emails and they got on well. She wrote the lyrics for this song after Adam emailed to say he was 'wonderstruck' to meet her. After the song was released Adam recorded his own version of it and sent it to Taylor with a note that called her a modern day Cinderella and that he was enchanted to meet her too. The album was originally going to be named after this track, before Taylor settled on *Speak Now*.

BETTER THAN REVENGE
Deviating from country pop, this track was influenced by pop punk, telling the story of a girl who Taylor said stole her boyfriend. She reportedly wrote the song when she was 18 after Joe Jonas broke up with her in favour of actress Camilla Belle. Taylor felt compelled to create a track inspired by the idea of revenge, but was criticised for the harsher 'anti-feminist' lyrics. In recent interviews, Taylor has said she now knows that partners can't be stolen from you if they don't want to leave.

LEFT: Taylor performing to crowds in her home state of Pennsylvania in 2011.

BELOW: During the Speak Now Tour, Taylor started her tradition of writing other artists' lyrics on her arm. "You've got every right to a beautiful life" is from the Selena Gomez song 'Who Says'.

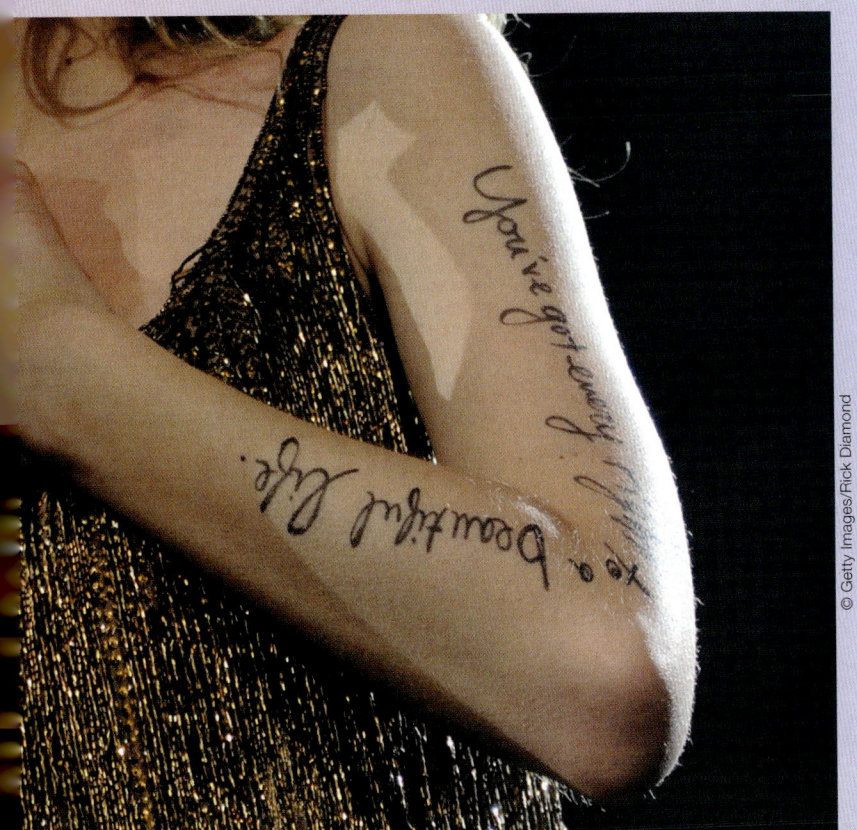

INNOCENT
Taylor described 'Innocent' as an open letter to somebody she forgave in front of the whole world. That statement coupled with a few clues in the lyrics suggest it's about Kanye West: "32, and still growing up now" (Kanye was 32 at the time of the 2009 VMAs). She thought it was only right to put it on this album. *Speak Now* is about figuring out how you feel and saying something about it. Some critics called it passive-aggressive while others called it beautiful. She performed this track for the very first time at the VMAs in 2010, one year after the Kanye West incident.

HAUNTED
Sometimes in a relationship one person starts to drift away and the love begins to fade. Taylor was going through this exact situation when she woke up in the middle of the night ready to write a song. Once she had the words she knew she needed to make the song a bit production to reflect its intensity. She recruited award-winning cellist and conductor Paul Buckmaster to add a string section to the track. Buckmaster had collaborated with legendary artists throughout his career from Celine Dion to David Bowie.

LAST KISS
Once again, Taylor used her life experience to pen this track. She was struck by the feelings of anger, frustration and confusion after a break-up and the utter sadness all of those feelings settle into. Rumour has it that 'Last Kiss' was written about Joe Jonas, but – true to form – Taylor has never confirmed nor denied this suspicion. The lyrics describe her reflections on the relationship, looking back on the good times that she didn't think would come to an end at the time. She admits to herself that there were a lot of emotions, hopes and memories she missed experiencing when she was in love.

LONG LIVE
The last song of the album is an anthem of victory. It's about all the moments of triumph and celebration of the first few years of her career. Taylor says it was a love song written to the team behind her. She wrote every single track on the album by herself but had a whole crew of people helping with its production and release, as well as the support from her millions of fans. She says all these people helped build her as an artist brick by brick and she wanted to share her success with them all.

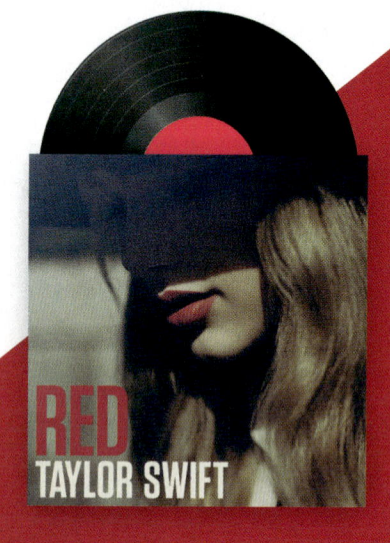

RED

RELEASED: 2012   **WORDS BY:** AMY GRISDALE

STEPPING FURTHER FROM HER COUNTRY ROOTS, TAYLOR'S FOURTH ALBUM FEATURED SUPERSTAR COLLABORATIONS AND VARIED MUSICAL STYLES

STATE OF GRACE

The first track of this album was released as the fourth single. Critics praised its broad style as almost all of her previous music had a lot of country influence. Taylor went on *Good Morning America* in October 2012 to give the world a sneak preview of the track. On the show she said the song was about the endless possibilities before you when you first fall in love. Viewers only heard a snippet of the chorus and had to wait more than a week for the 16-track album to come out in full.

RED

Taylor uses colours to express different emotions in this song. She said that the two years leading up to this album were full of crazy and tumultuous feelings and she was inspired by that intensity. She sang about the colour blue being the feeling of losing a lover and dark grey described the feeling of missing him. Red was what she felt when she loved him. She was praised by critics for honesty and heart in the lyrics as well as the musicality and production of the song.

© Getty Images/Kevin Mazur/WireImage

22

Despite massive success in songwriting and performing, Taylor sometimes found critics still dismissed her music because of her youth. This track flaunted her youth in the face of her older critics with a new bubblegum pop sound. She has stated in interviews that being 22 taught her a lot about letting loose in the face of fear and indecision. She said it's an age where you are aware that you don't have much life experience and that there are a lot of life lessons ahead. This is the time to enjoy being carefree even if it's only for a short while.

I ALMOST DO

Going back to her Nashville roots with a heavy country feel, Taylor penned this song unassisted and had a hand in additional production on the finished track. The song expresses Taylor's feelings of missing a former partner who remains anonymous. The lyrics discuss loneliness and a near-irresistible urge to pick up the phone and talk to him: "I just want to tell you, it takes everything in me not to call you [...] Every time I don't, I almost do". She wonders if he's thinking about her and says that even though their relationship was messy she dreams about it and almost wishes they were still together.

ABOVE: Snow Patrol singer Gary Lightbody co-wrote and sang the hit single 'The Last Time' with Taylor.

LEFT: Performing 'We Are Never Ever Getting Back Together' at the MTV EMAs in 2012, where Taylor won Best Female Artist, Best Live Act and Best Look.

ALL TOO WELL

Taylor said this track was the most difficult to compose on the whole album. It began with her playing the chords over and over and ranting about the hardship she was experiencing. She had to filter the elements down or she would have ended up with a 20-minute song that nobody would have listened to. She recruited long-time writing partner Liz Rose to help prune away the less important parts. Even with two expert writers chopping it down it still came out as the longest track on the album at five minutes and 28 seconds.

TREACHEROUS

This track is about a relationship in Taylor's life that she knew would end badly. She said it had a magnetic draw that didn't allow her to escape the heartbreak. The song received huge critical acclaim for maintaining the high standard of quality in the previous album, *Speak Now*. The verses were praised for their 'hushed, confessional beauty' and critics wrote that Taylor's vocals were going from strength to strength. Taylor collaborated with Dan Wilson of the band Semisonic who had previously worked with Adele on her song 'Someone Like You'.

I KNEW YOU WERE TROUBLE

This was one of Taylor's favourite songs on the entire album because it reflects the chaos she felt when writing it. People speculate that it was written about John Mayer but Taylor has declined to comment on the subject of the song. She composed it on her own and the media loved its mainstream appeal with the added touch of dubstep in the chorus. It became her 14th top 10 hit and made Taylor the first artist in digital history to debut two songs with more than 400,000 sales. It earned her another VMA for Best Female Video and won another four awards of the nine for which it was nominated.

WE ARE NEVER EVER GETTING BACK TOGETHER

This break-up anthem was the first single to be released from *Red* and topped the charts around the world. Having written her previous album solo she was keen to work with other artists again. She invited two Swedish musicians, Max Martin and Shellback, to collaborate on a new track. She had heard rumours that she was getting back together with an old flame from a friend. Max and Shellback asked for the details and Taylor told them about their dynamic of splitting up and reuniting and the lyrics of the song flowed naturally from there.

STAY STAY STAY
As the title suggests, this one is about pleading with a lover to remain in the relationship with her. The press criticised her for putting out so many songs about love and heartbreak in a short time. Taylor's songs are popular because they are full of her honest emotions and *Red* is about the rollercoaster ride she felt she was on throughout writing the album. The writing itself was draining as she had to hop from emotional lows when writing more mournful tracks to singing about how amazing it is to meet somebody new.

THE LAST TIME
Snow Patrol singer Gary Lightbody joined in with the writing and performance of the final single from *Red*. The alternative rock duet was produced by Jacknife Lee who is famous for working with bands like Snow Patrol and U2. The lyrics tell the story of a long-term relationship that is crumbling away piece by piece, with Swift's character granting Lightbody's character one final chance to salvage things between them. It was dubbed the most mature track on the album by critics.

HOLY GROUND
The lyrics of this track describe a difficult relationship that ended quickly, but the two are on good terms now. It's believed to be about Joe Jonas, but we don't know for sure. The song says that they had a brief period of perfection together before the couple split up, and in those good times everywhere they stepped together was 'holy ground'. The song was produced by Jeff Bhasker who also worked on Kanye West's fifth album.

SAD BEAUTIFUL TRAGIC
This doesn't seem to be about one particular person but fans guess either John Mayer of Jake Gyllenhaal. Taylor wrote it sitting in her tour bus after a live show when she found herself thinking about an old relationship. She realised she wasn't sad or angry any more but felt a distinct wistful loss. She wanted the song to be a little bit ambiguous to mirror the murkiness of her memories of her past relationship. Taylor wanted her album to be all over the place like her feelings.

RIGHT: Taylor wrote and performed the duet 'Everything Has Changed' with her friend Ed Sheeran.

THE LUCKY ONE
In this song Taylor addresses her fears of falling into obscurity. The lyrics talk about a star who has everything but cannot handle the pressure of constant media attention. There's speculation about the identity of the celebrity in the song but it could be Kim Wilde. Taylor sampled her song 'Four Letter Word' in 'The Lucky One' and refers to giving up performing to work in a rose garden (Kim Wilde left the spotlight and became a landscape gardener). The song ends with Taylor saying that she understands why the star chose that path.

EVERYTHING HAS CHANGED
Rumours were flying about Ed Sheeran appearing on this album for months before its release. They wrote this song together sitting out in Taylor's back garden and worked well as a team. Ed Sheeran claims that when they disagreed over a chord he bowed to Taylor's superior knowledge. The core concept of the song is how everything can seem completely different when you enter a new relationship. She says the impact of that particular person coming into your life is powerful and exciting and in the song she's eager to get to know them better.

STARLIGHT
Taylor came across an old photo of human rights advocate Ethel Kennedy and her husband Robert 'Bobby' F Kennedy. The photo was of the pair dancing at the age of 17 back in the 1940s. Taylor was so inspired by it that she decided to write a song about their relationship despite not knowing exactly how they got together. A few weeks later she bumped into one of Ethel and Robert's 11 children and had the chance to meet Ethel in person. Tragically Robert, like his brother John F Kennedy, was assassinated in the 1960s.

BEGIN AGAIN
Because so much of the album deviated from her traditional style it's only right that *Red* ends with a country ballad. Taylor sings about a girl braving a first date with a new man after getting over a bad relationship. A girl in that situation can feel so vulnerable and the song encourages girls to be bold. In the song she talks about having things in common with the new man, including the music of James Taylor (after whom Taylor was named): "You said you never met one girl who had as many James Taylor records as you, but I do."

Taylor on the opening night of The Red Tour in March 2013. *Red* was seen as her transitional album between country and pop.

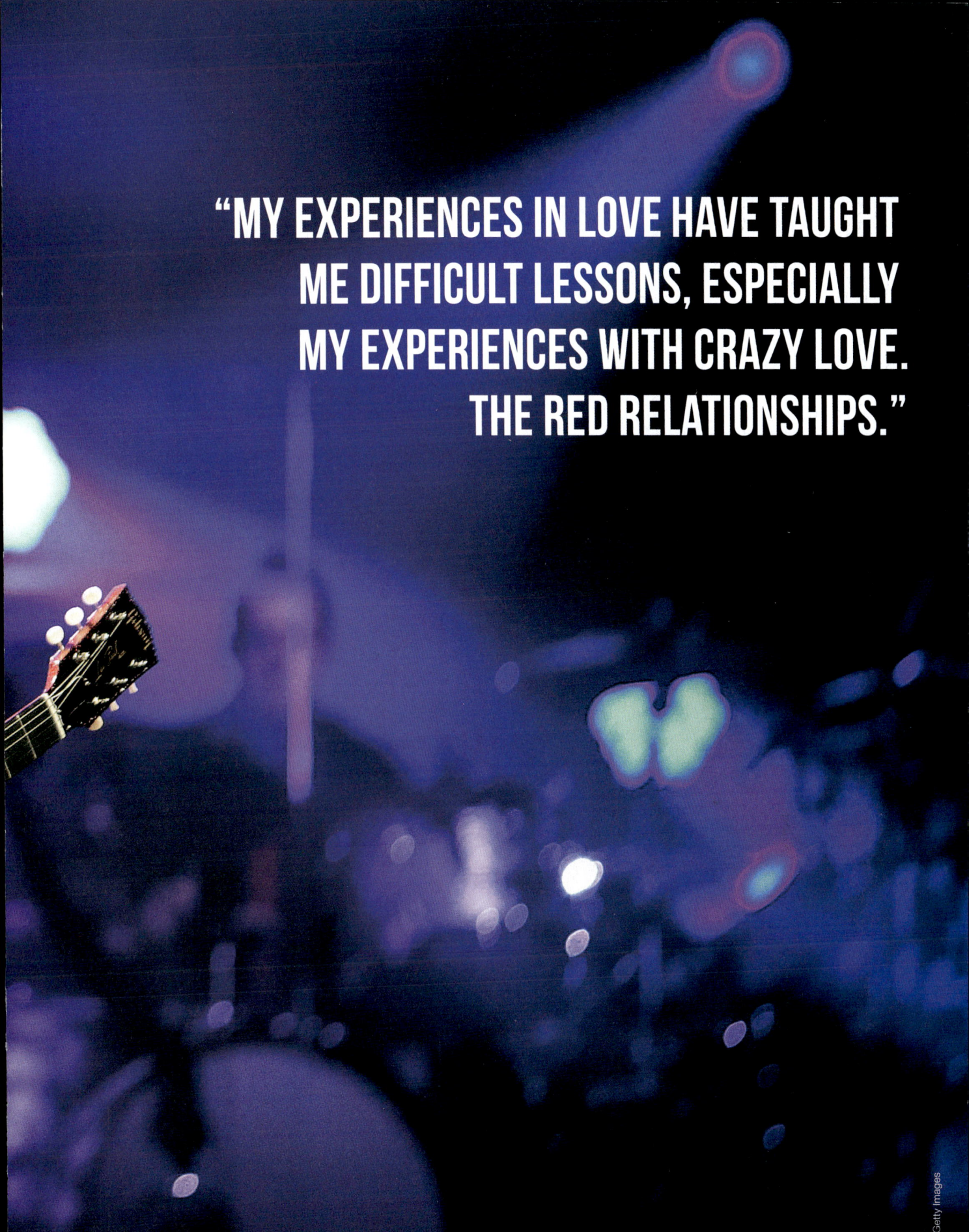

"MY EXPERIENCES IN LOVE HAVE TAUGHT ME DIFFICULT LESSONS, ESPECIALLY MY EXPERIENCES WITH CRAZY LOVE. THE RED RELATIONSHIPS."

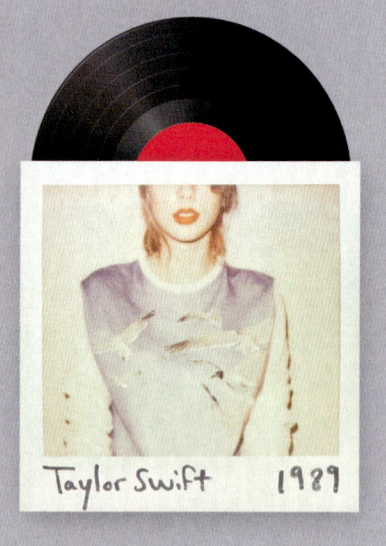

1989

RELEASED: 2014   **WORDS BY:** HANNAH WALES

AFTER FLIRTING WITH POP ON **RED**, TAYLOR MOVED AWAY FROM COUNTRY MUSIC ALTOGETHER AND ESTABLISHED HERSELF AS A FULL-FLEDGED POP STAR WITH **1989**

WELCOME TO NEW YORK
The album's opening track celebrates the endless possibilities available to people in New York City, where Taylor moved in 2014. She wrote the song with Ryan Tedder from OneRepublic, and wanted it to be the first track on the album because her relocation had such a big impact on her life around that time. The lyrics: "And you can want who you want, boys and boys and girls and girls" was interpreted as Taylor's shout out in support of the LGBTQ+ community.

BLANK SPACE
On the album's second single, Taylor pokes fun at the media's perception of her and her relationship history, with lyrics such as, "I'm a nightmare dressed like a daydream" and "Got a long list of ex-lovers, they'll tell you I'm insane." She creates a character that is an exaggeration of the man-eater she was portrayed to be in the media at that time. The electro-pop track also marks her first of many collaborations with Swedish pop music extraordinaires Max Martin and Shellback.

> "THESE SONGS WERE ONCE ABOUT MY LIFE. NOW THEY ARE ABOUT YOURS."

STYLE

Style is one of Taylor's more ambiguous tracks. While it may seem like a song about timeless style and fashion, with references to 1950s movie star James Dean and a classic red lip, the lyrics actually depict an unhealthy on-off relationship. Taylor sings about knowing they should finally call it quits yet they can't help crawling back to each other. Many fans interpreted the song to be about her ex-boyfriend Harry Styles, thanks to the lyrics: "You've got that long hair, slicked back, white T-shirt."

OUT OF THE WOODS

On the sixth single off *1989*, Taylor looks back at a fragile, unstable relationship. The track contains the extremely specific lyrics: "Remember when you hit the brakes too soon, 20 stitches in a hospital room," a reference to a serious snowmobile accident she was involved in with an ex-boyfriend which nobody knew about until the song was released. Fans believe the ex in question to be Styles due to the lyrics: "Your necklace hanging round my neck [...] Two papers airplanes flying," an apparent reference to the matching necklaces they once wore.

LEFT: Several tracks on the album are thought to refer to Taylor's relationship with Harry Styles.

ABOVE: Some BFFs from the 'Bad Blood' video (L-R): Zendaya, Hailee Steinfeld, Taylor Swift, Lily Aldridge and Martha Hunt.

ALL YOU HAD TO DO WAS STAY

In this song, Taylor sings directly to an ex who has come back on the scene after ending their relationship, and she has no interest in taking him back. She recalls how he locked her out and "drove us off the road" and firmly tells him he's too late and she's done with him, singing: "People like me are gone forever when you say goodbye." The track also features the recurring high-pitched yell "Stay!" throughout, which was inspired by a dream she had about an ex showing up at her door and that's the only sound that would come out of her mouth. 'All You Had To Do Was Stay' also follows Taylor's tradition of making the fifth track on her albums the most emotional.

SHAKE IT OFF

'Shake It Off' was the lead single from *1989* and made the clear statement that Taylor was now a full-on pop star. The uptempo dance-pop track, written with Martin and Shellback, addresses the rumours and misconceptions about her life and how she brushes them off and pays no attention to them so she can enjoy herself.

The opening verse references the media portrayal of Taylor as a 'serial dater' ("I go on too many dates, but I can't make them stay, at least that's what people say.") While she makes light of it in the song, Taylor has often spoken about her frustrations with the media's obsession with her love life.

I WISH YOU WOULD

This song opens with a guy driving down a street in the middle of the night and he passes his ex-girlfriend's house. He assumes she hates him when she's actually still in love with him. Taylor directly addresses the ex and wishes she could go back in time and handle their rough patches differently, with lyrics like, "Wish I'd never hung up the phone like I did," and "I wish you knew that I'd never forget you as long as I live." She wrote the lyrics to a track Jack Antonoff had created, in a similar fashion to 'Out Of The Woods'.

BAD BLOOD

The context of this song is probably the most well-known from *1989*, exploring Taylor's feud with Katy Perry. The song describes a betrayal by a close friend, and Taylor later clarified that it was about a female musician who tried to sabotage one of her tours by hiring some of her dancers. Although she didn't point fingers, it was quickly reported that Taylor was singing about losing her friendship with the 'Firework' singer. Their feud rumbled on for many years and they finally buried the hatchet in 2018. A remixed version of the track, featuring a reworked instrumental and vocals by Kendrick Lamar on the verses, was released as the fourth single off *1989* and was accompanied by a very star-studded music video.

WILDEST DREAMS

Slower than most of the tracks on the album, 'Wildest Dreams', the album's fifth single, has a sultry, dream-like quality that sparked comparisons to Lana Del Rey's work. In the track, Taylor hopes that her lover will always remember her and the good memories they shared once they are over, and while she hopes it lasts, she knows it won't, with her singing: "I can see the ends as it begins" and "Someday when you leave me, I'd bet these memories follow you around."

RIGHT: Taylor performing in front of fans in Sydney, Australia during her 1989 World Tour.

> "I LISTENED TO A LOT OF MUSIC FROM THE DECADE IN WHICH I WAS BORN."

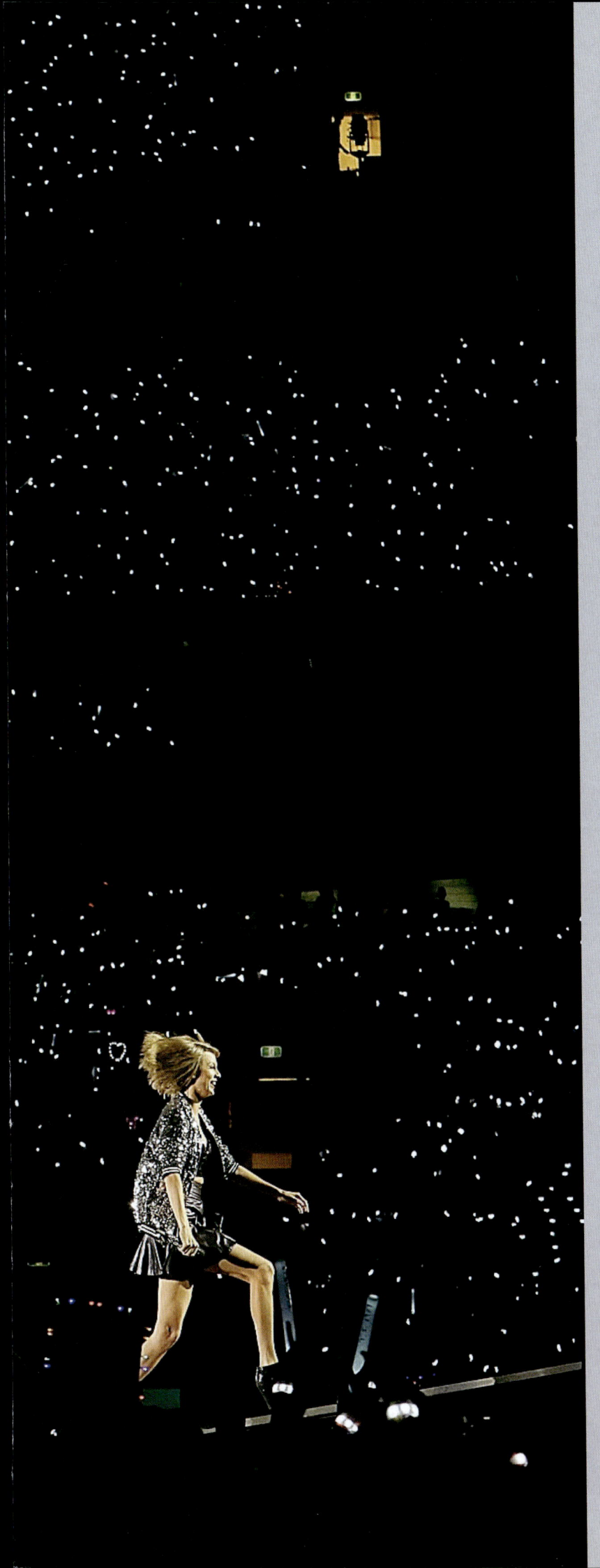

HOW YOU GET THE GIRL
In this upbeat pop track, Taylor offers advice to a guy to help him win his ex back after he broke her heart by leaving without explanation six months before. She suggests ways to get back into the girl's good books and offers up recommendations of what to say, shown in lyrics such as, "Say it's been a long six months, and you were too afraid to tell her what you want." By the end of the song, Taylor's advice has been successful and the guy and girl in question are back together.

THIS LOVE
This slow and soft ballad sounds very different from the rest of 1989 and that's because it's the only track to be written solely by Taylor. It also marks her reunion with Nathan Chapman, who produced many songs on her country-era albums. With her breathy, relaxing vocals, Taylor sings about the cyclical nature of a relationship – the good and the bad parts of it – and how a lover comes in and out of her life. The chorus, which ends with: "This love came back to me," began as a short poem Taylor wrote in her journal following a real-life event and she immediately heard the melody and knew it had to be a song.

I KNOW PLACES
In this track, Taylor sings about the effect fame has on a relationship and how difficult it is for a high-profile couple to maintain a private life. She uses a metaphor of a fox hunt, where they are the foxes and the media are the hunters, and speaks to a new lover to reassure them that she knows where they can go without anyone noticing ("They'll be chasing their tails trying to track us down"). Taylor had the melody and majority of the lyrics down before a studio session with Tedder, and they completed and recorded it the following day.

CLEAN
Taylor created this emotional ballad with Imogen Heap, who co-wrote the track, played the instruments, and sang background vocals. The song focuses on Taylor realising she is finally over a relationship and no longer heartbroken. She uses water imagery to illustrate the point, as the song opens with a drought, presumably symbolising the end of the relationship, before there is a gathering storm and then a downpour, which leaves her completely clean. Although the song was intended to be about love, some of the lyrics can be interpreted as a reference to addiction, such as, "Ten months sober, I must admit, just because you're clean don't mean you don't miss it."

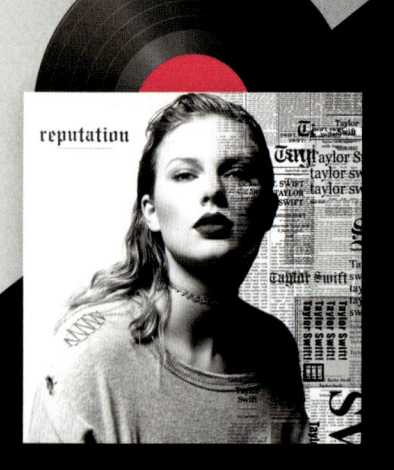

REPUTATION

RELEASED: 2017   WORDS BY: HANNAH WALES

MAKING A DEPARTURE FROM HER USUAL SUNNY DISPOSITION, TAYLOR RETURNED FROM HER TIME OUT OF THE SPOTLIGHT WITH A DARKER SOUND ON **REPUTATION**

...READY FOR IT?
In the second single, Taylor takes on the persona of a robber who is "stealing hearts and running off and never sayin' sorry." She meets her perfect partner in crime who will "join the heist" and escape to an island with her. The song seems to be a reference to Joe Alwyn as she describes him as "younger than my exes" and states how their love is different to her other romances, with her rapping: "Every love I've known in comparison is a failure." The song features sexually suggestive lyrics, Taylor rapping in the verses, and references to classic Hollywood couple Richard Burton and Elizabeth Taylor.

END GAME
Taylor reunited with Ed Sheeran, her duet partner on 2012 track 'Everything Has Changed', once again for 'End Game', which also features a verse from rapper Future. 'End Game' focuses on Taylor wanting a lover to be the person she ends up with for the rest of her life, with her singing that she doesn't want to be "just another ex-love you don't wanna see." In the track, Taylor acknowledges her "reputation precedes" her and assumes her lover has already been told she's 'crazy'.

I DID SOMETHING BAD
Just like 'Blank Space', Taylor leans into the character she was given by the media and public and sings from that perspective, with the chorus containing the lyrics: "They say I did something bad, but why's it feel so good? Most fun I ever had, and I'd do it over and over and over again if I could." This song features heavy electronic and trap elements, as well as an expletive – a rare occurrence in her music. The post-chorus effect was created using Taylor's pitched-down voice as producer Martin couldn't find an instrument to achieve the sound she wanted. This song is thought to make reference to rival Kanye West and her ex-boyfriend Calvin Harris.

DON'T BLAME ME
In this midtempo track, Taylor compares being in love with Alwyn to a drug addiction, with her singing that love has made her crazy, and "My drug is my baby, I'll be usin' for the rest of my life." She continues the metaphor in the bridge when she sings "I get so high" and describes their romance as the "trip of my life". She also continues to play into the media's perception of her love life as she sings about "Toyin' with them older guys, just playthings for me to use." Many fans and critics have noted its sonic similarities to Hozier's 'Take Me to Church'.

DELICATE

Taylor sounds remarkably different on Delicate, the sixth single, as she used a vocoder to give her voice a vulnerable and emotional quality, marking the first time she expresses vulnerability on the album. In all the tracks before 'Delicate', Swift is strong and feisty, telling listeners she doesn't care about what people say about her, but in this, she questions how her reputation will affect the beginning of a new relationship, presumably with Alwyn, and wonders how much he's already heard about her and if it will cloud his judgement. Key lyrics include: "My reputation's never been worse, so you must like me for me."

LOOK WHAT YOU MADE ME DO

The album's lead single was a huge departure from any of Swift's previous music and firmly established her new darker sound. Taylor used the track to declare she was a new person, thanks to the lyrics: "The old Taylor can't come to the phone right now. Why? Oh, 'cause she's dead!" The song appears to reference her feud with West and the damage done to her reputation as a result of it, with lyrics such as, "I don't trust nobody and nobody trusts me." Members of British band Right Said Fred are credited as songwriters because her repetitive, almost-spoken chorus incorporates the melody of their 1991 song 'I'm Too Sexy'.

SO IT GOES...

This is one of the more sexually suggestive songs in Taylor's back catalogue, with lyrics including: "I'm not a bad girl, but I'll do bad things with you" and "Scratches down your back now..." It is thought to be about Alwyn, with the lyrics describing how they only have eyes for each other and get "caught up in a moment" when they're together, but "break down a little" when they're apart.

GORGEOUS

The album's fifth single marks Taylor's return to her more conventional upbeat pop sound and opens with James, the daughter of Ryan Reynolds and Blake Lively, saying the word 'gorgeous'. The song is about her having a crush on Alwyn even though she was in a relationship with somebody else when they met, with the lyrics explaining: "And I got a boyfriend, he's older than us, he's in the club doing, I don't know what." Despite her relationship status, she's annoyed she's not with Alwyn, as she sings: "You've ruined my life, by not being mine."

GETAWAY CAR

In this track, Taylor uses the imagery of criminals escaping a crime scene in a getaway car as a metaphor for a romance that was doomed from the start. The lyrics can be interpreted as a reference to her short-lived rebound romance with actor Tom Hiddleston, with her likening him to a getaway car speeding her away from her relationship with Calvin Harris. She knew the romance didn't have a real shot because of how it began, with her singing: "Should've known I'd be the first to leave, think about the place where you first met me."

KING OF MY HEART

The song has a unique structure as each section of it depicts the progression of a relationship, with the first verse describing Taylor being happy on her own before Alwyn comes along, the pre-chorus representing the couple being in love, and the chorus showing their love getting deeper and more serious, with the lyrics: "And all at once, you're all I want, I'll never let you go, king of my heart, body, and soul." The accompanying music also radically changes throughout each stage. Taylor was influenced by *Game of Thrones* when she wrote *reputation* and wanted the post-chorus drum beat to sound like Dothraki drums.

DANCING WITH OUR HANDS TIED

This song depicts the early stages of Taylor's relationship with Alwyn, when she loved him "in secret" and the public didn't know about it yet. Much like 'I Know Places' on *1989*, this track details her fears about fame and the scrutiny surrounding her life ruining the romance once it gets discovered. Key lyrics include: "People started talking, putting us through our paces, I knew there was no one in the world who could take it, I had a bad feeling." The lyrics used in the title suggest they are having fun but lack the freedom and control that a normal couple would have.

LEFT: Taylor and Kanye's feud is thought to have inspired the track 'Look What You Made Me Do'.

reputation was thematically much darker than Taylor's previous albums.

> "WE THINK WE KNOW SOMEONE, BUT THE TRUTH IS THAT WE ONLY KNOW THE VERSION OF THEM THEY HAVE CHOSEN TO SHOW US."

DRESS
'Dress' is perhaps the most overtly sexual song Taylor has ever written, with her revealing that she only brought the dress mentioned in the title so her man would take it off. The line, "I don't want you like a best friend," sparked a lot of debate regarding the subject of the song, with Sheeran being the prime suspect, but the track is once again about Alwyn. It seems to depict the stage in their relationship when they transitioned from friends to lovers, but nobody else knew, and she seemingly struggled to keep her attraction to him a secret.

THIS IS WHY WE CAN'T HAVE NICE THINGS
This light-hearted track opens with Taylor referring to the star-studded parties she used to throw for her 'squad' before the media turned on her for them. It also features one of the most specific references to her feud with West and his wife Kim Kardashian – "Friends don't try to trick you, get you on the phone and mind-twist you" – and touches upon her ruined reputation, with her praising her "real friends" and boyfriend for paying no attention to the gossip. She adds a comic touch by laughing after singing the words, "'Cause forgiveness is a nice thing to do" and saying, "I can't even say it with a straight face", suggesting she hadn't actually forgiven the rapper.

CALL IT WHAT YOU WANT
This slow spare ballad is set in the months Taylor stepped out of the public eye in 2016. Although her reputation was in tatters, she was doing just fine because she was falling in love with Alwyn, and the criticism "fades to nothing" when she's with him. The most poignant lyrics include: "My castle crumbled overnight" and "all the liars are calling me one," which refers to her public fall from grace. However, despite this, she insists, "I'm doing better than I ever was" due to her new romance.

NEW YEAR'S DAY
In contrast to the electro-pop that dominates the record, New Year's Day is a simple piano-led ballad. It is set the day after a big New Year's Eve party and features Taylor singing about being there to kiss Alwyn at midnight and also to clear up the mess the following day, meaning they will be both there during each other's highs and lows. Taylor can tell it's going "to be a long road" with him and hopes it doesn't ever come to an end, with the most telling lyrics including: "Please don't ever become a stranger whose laugh I could recognise anywhere."

LOVER

RELEASED: 2019   WORDS BY: HANNAH WALES

SWIFT'S SEVENTH ALBUM WAS A CELEBRATION OF LOVE AND MARKED A RETURN TO A HAPPIER AND MORE UPBEAT SOUND

I FORGOT THAT YOU EXISTED
In the opening track, Taylor makes it clear that she has drawn a line under the events that inspired the dark tone of *reputation*. She recalls how much time she spent thinking about the person who had wronged her, presumably referring to Kanye West, and how she "lived in the shade you were throwing, til all of my sunshine was gone." She has found that her life is much better now she's let it go and considers that person with indifference. The carefree, upbeat song has a minimalist arrangement, with the vocals being accompanied by short piano chords and finger clicks.

CRUEL SUMMER
In this breezy pop track, Taylor sings about falling in love with a "bad boy" she is having a casual summer fling with. She is uncertain about the future of the relationship and is desperately pining for something more. In the bridge, she finally confesses her feelings in the lyrics: "And I scream, 'For whatever it's worth, I love you, ain't that the worst thing you ever heard?'" This is presumably about the beginning of her relationship with Joe Alwyn, as the man in the song grins in response to her declaration. The music was written by Jack Antonoff in collaboration with Annie Clark (aka St. Vincent).

LOVER
The album's title track and third single is a slow, romantic waltz with a nostalgic, timeless feel. Taylor wrote the acoustic guitar-led ballad, which describes her love for Alwyn, on her own the night before a studio session with Antonoff and they wanted to accompany the confessional lyrics with music that could have been played at a '70s wedding reception. The lyrics in the bridge sound similar to wedding vows, with the lines: "Ladies and gentlemen, will you please stand? […] I take this magnetic force of a man to be my lover."

ABOVE: Fans believe that many of the tracks on *Lover* refer to Taylor's relationship with Joe Alwyn.

TOP RIGHT: Taylor spent up to six hours in make-up for her transformation into 'Tyler Swift' for the music video of 'The Man', which she also directed.

THE MAN
In the album's fourth single, Taylor addresses the sexism and double standards she has experienced during her career. She imagines how differently she would have been perceived and treated by the press and the public if she had been a man – and made the same choices in her life – with key lyrics including: "I'd be fearless leader, I'd be an alpha type, to have everyone believe you, what's that like?"

THE ARCHER
'The Archer' is a deeply personal and honest song, in keeping with her tradition of making her most vulnerable work the fifth track of each album. It is a spare and minimalist midtempo song featuring heavy synths and soft house beats which build to create a sense of urgency, and in the poetic lyrics, Taylor reflects on her flaws in past relationships and her insecurities about her current one. She acknowledges that she has been both the archer and the prey and asks: "Who could ever leave me, darling, but who could stay?" It also makes a reference to the nursery rhyme Humpty Dumpty as she sings: "All the king's horses, all the king's men, couldn't put me together again."

"THIS ALBUM IS A LOVE LETTER TO LOVE ITSELF."

I THINK HE KNOWS
In this track, Taylor sings about her attraction to Alwyn, revealing that her infatuation makes her feel like 17 years old again. She sings about how they're mutually obsessed with each other, and she feels as though she's "an architect, I'm drawing up the plans" of their lives, and she doesn't need to tell him how much she's into him because he already knows. The line "He got my heartbeat skipping down 16th Avenue" refers to Music Row in Nashville, where Taylor used to write songs earlier in her career. The song begins with minimalist production, as Taylor's vocals are delivered against a simple backing track of clicks before hitting a catchy, funk-inspired groove at the chorus.

MISS AMERICANA & THE HEARTBREAK PRINCE
'Miss Americana', which inspired the name of her Netflix documentary, is set in a high school. Its slow, melancholic production is peppered with cheerleader chants and seems, on the surface, to tell the story of a high school romance, reminiscent of 'You Belong With Me'. However, Taylor wrote it shortly after the 2018 US midterm elections to express her disappointment in the state of US politics. This is best exemplified with the lyrics: "American glory, faded before me," and "I saw the scoreboard, and ran for my life." She makes it clear that she supports the Democrats with the line, "We're so sad, we paint the town blue" and ends on a hopeful note, as she's determined her team is going to win one day.

PAPER RINGS

In this bubbly and upbeat pop song, Taylor considers how far her and Alwyn have come from the beginning of their relationship, when she initially gave him the cold shoulder. She reminisces about the fun memories they share, reaffirms her commitment to him, and confesses that even though she likes "shiny things", she'd be so willing to marry him that she would do it with homemade paper rings.

CORNELIA STREET

In the opening verse, Taylor sings, "'I rent a place on Cornelia Street,' I say casually in the car", referring to the apartment she briefly rented in Greenwich Village in 2016. The song, which Taylor wrote on her own, is about her never wanting a relationship to end and how she would never be able to walk down that street again if they broke up as it would bring back all the memories she has connected with the place. Towards the end of the song, windscreen wipers can be heard in the background, helping listeners conjure up the image of them in the car.

RIGHT: Taylor won the Best Direction award for 'The Man' at the 2020 VMAs. She accepted it remotely due to the pandemic.

BELOW: The planned Lover Fest tour had to be postponed due to the Covid-19 pandemic.

DEATH BY A THOUSAND CUTS

With this track, Taylor wanted to prove that she could still write a break-up song despite being in a loving relationship. Instead of using a moment from her own life, she was inspired by the characters and dynamics in the 2019 Netflix film *Someone Great*, which follows a woman who is trying to cope with heartbreak after getting dumped by her long-term boyfriend. Taylor admitted the film affected her so much that she started having dreams about living through the same situation. She wrote the lyrics on her own before bringing them to a studio session with Antonoff.

LONDON BOY

This light-hearted song opens with a snippet of Idris Elba talking about driving around London on his scooter, which was taken from his appearance on *The Late Late Show* with James Corden. The track serves as a celebration of her "London boy", meaning Alwyn, and details some of their favourite things to do in the British capital, with her naming places such as Brixton, Highgate, Camden Market and Shoreditch, singing about watching rugby in a pub, using slang such as "mate" and "babes", and namechecking fashion designer Stella McCartney, who she worked with on a line of *Lover* merchandise. The track interpolates the rhythm from Cautious Clay's *Cold War*, so he is credited as a songwriter.

SOON YOU'LL GET BETTER
This extremely emotional and personal ballad is about Taylor's mother's second battle with cancer. Taylor rarely sings about her family and was unsure about including this on the album. In the song, she repeats to her mum that she'll get better "'Cause you have to", but it's as if she's trying to convince them both, wondering how she'll cope if her mum isn't around anymore. This track also features backing vocals from Taylor's country idols, The Chicks.

FALSE GOD
False God is a sensual R&B-influenced love song featuring a solo saxophone throughout. Taylor uses heavy religious imagery to describe the ups and downs in her relationship with Alwyn and how their love might be a false God, but they'd still worship it anyway. Notable lyrics include: "The altar is my hips" and "Make confessions and we're begging for forgiveness, got the wine for you."

YOU NEED TO CALM DOWN
Taylor takes a clear stand with the LGBTQ+ community in *Lover*'s second single, which is directed at internet trolls and homophobes. To those who waste energy writing hateful messages to strangers, she sings: "'Cause shade never made anybody less gay [...] You need to just stop." She was inspired to write the song with Joel Little after realising that her support for the LGBTQ+ community hadn't been loud or obvious enough.

AFTERGLOW
In this track, Taylor recalls having a heated fight with her partner, apologises for hurting his feelings and asks for reassurance that he won't leave her, "even when I lose my mind". She takes responsibility for blowing something out of proportion, punishing him with silence and for being the one who "burned us down" and asks for forgiveness. Key lyrics include: "I don't want to do this to you" and "I don't want to lose this with you."

ME!
This bubblegum pop song served as the lead single from *Lover* and reaffirmed Taylor's return to a more cheerful and upbeat tone. 'ME!' is all about embracing self-love, celebrating and owning your individuality. It is a duet between Taylor and Brendon Urie from Panic! at the Disco, who have both been fans of each other's work for years. They sing from both sides of a couple, each insisting the other will never do any better, with lyrics like: "I promise that you'll never find another like me."

IT'S NICE TO HAVE A FRIEND
This dreamy love ballad could be seen as a story of two childhood friends who embark on a romance and end up getting married, however, Taylor has clarified that it is about the feeling of finding a close friend at different times of your life, rather than one linear story. It begins with Taylor being nostalgic about childhood friendships and then comparing them to finding a friend in the person you love. This track is very different from Taylor's usual output in terms of instrumentation, as her vocals are accompanied by steel drums and harps (giving the song an almost music-box quality), as well as a trumpet solo and a choir of background vocals. It also samples 'Summer in the South', a track by The Regent Park School of Music youth choir in Toronto, Canada.

DAYLIGHT
Taylor considered calling the album *Daylight* for a while, but eventually went with *Lover*. She chose the ballad, which she wrote on her own, as the album's closing track because it recognises the past damage and pain she's experienced in relationships and the fact that she's finally decided to let it all go so she can experience the daylight with Alwyn. Forgiving herself for past mistakes, she sings: "I wounded the good and I trusted the wicked." It features a callback to her song 'Red' and concludes with a spoken word outro in which Taylor says she wants "to be defined by the things that I love."

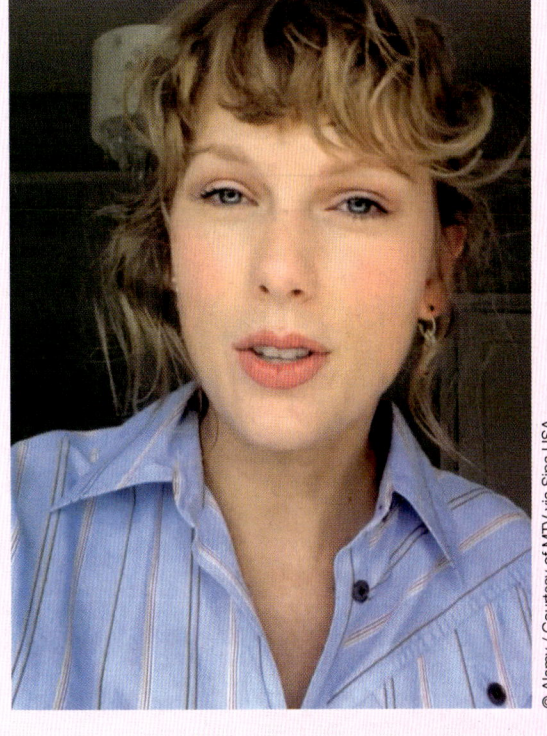

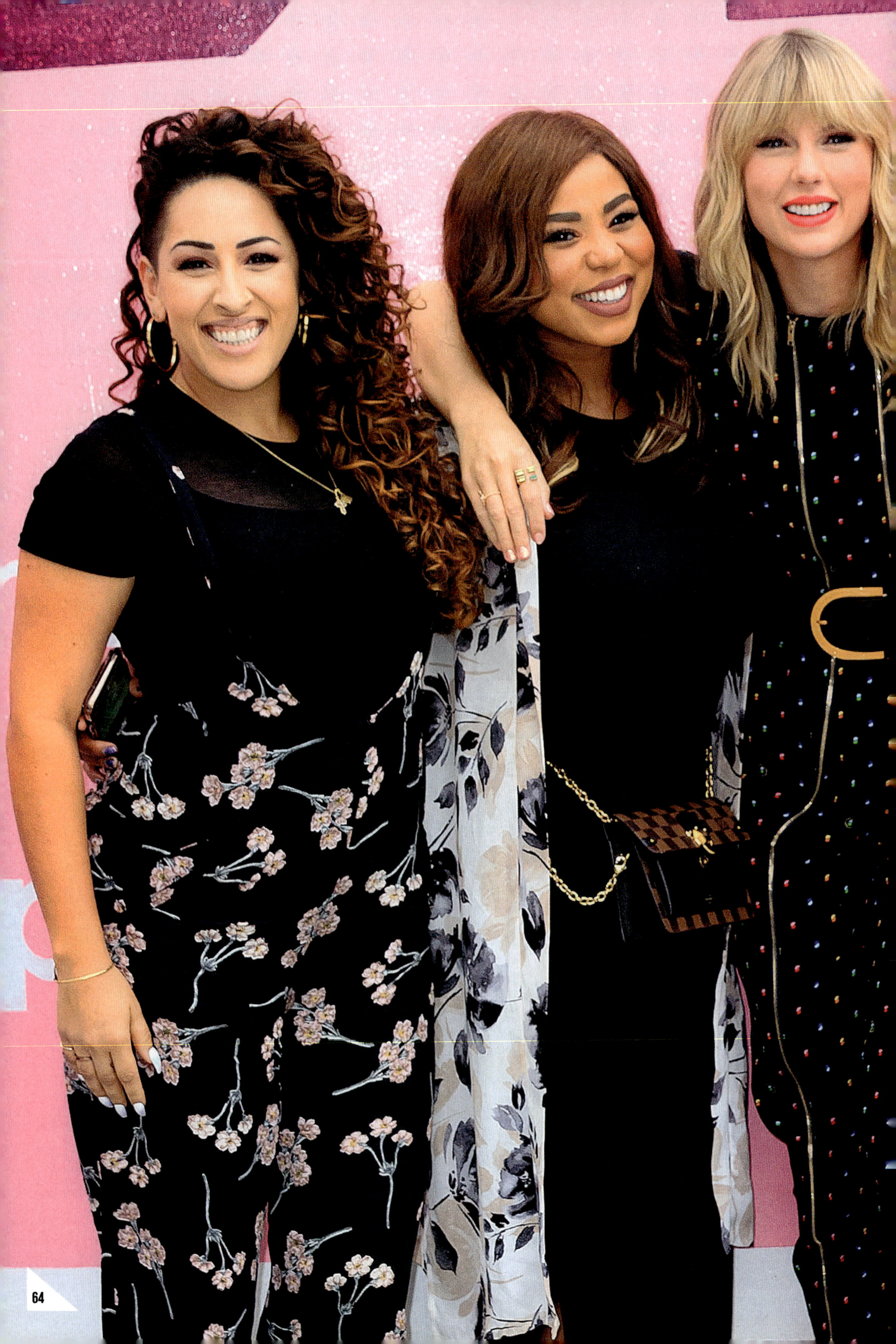

Taylor posing with her backing singers Jeslyn Gorman, Eliotte Nicole, Melanie Nyema and Kamilah Marshall at a press event for *Lover*.

FOLKLORE

RELEASED: JULY 2020

TAYLOR'S SURPRISE LOCKDOWN ALBUM SEES HER EFFORTLESSLY SWITCH GEAR ONCE AGAIN, LEAVING POP BEHIND TO PRODUCE A WISTFUL, MELANCHOLIC MASTERPIECE

the 1

The opening track sees Taylor contemplating a past relationship. While the verses are more upbeat – as Taylor appreciates the good things she has and wishes her ex well – this positive outlook soon morphs into nostalgia and thoughts of 'what if' during the chorus: "If one thing had been different, would everything be different today?" Taylor's *folklore* collaborator, Aaron Dessner (of The National), revealed in an interview with *Vulture* that this track was actually a late addition: "'the 1' and 'hoax' were the last songs we did. The album was sort of finished before that [...] These are the bookends, you know?"

cardigan

The first single from *folklore* is an enchanting piano ballad, and also the first of what Taylor calls the Teenage Love Triangle, a collection of interconnected tracks exploring a fictional high-school romance from each person's point of view. Alongside 'august' and 'betty', 'cardigan' tells the story from Betty's perspective as she reflects on her relationship with James. Despite being heartbroken after he cheats on her, Betty believes he'll return to her: "I knew you'd miss me once the thrill expired, and you'd be standing in my front porch light. And I knew you'd come back to me..." – an event that's revisited from James' perspective later in the album.

the last great american dynasty

This song describes the life of Rebekah Harkness, a wealthy heiress and patron of the arts whose eccentric behaviour earned her an infamous reputation in high society. It is one of the more uptempo tracks on the album, with a jaunty syncopated beat driving the melody along. As the song progresses, the story becomes personal as Taylor draws parallels between Harkness and herself. Several years ago, Taylor bought the heiress' old Rhode Island mansion, Holiday House, and both women have received their unfair share of scrutiny from the media. Tongue in cheek, she triumphantly sings through the outro, "I had a marvellous time ruining everything."

LEFT: In November 2020, Taylor released the documentary concert film *folklore: the long pond studio sessions* on Disney+ to accompany the album.

RIGHT: The video for 'cardigan' was made with strict Covid-19 guidelines in place – Taylor did her own hair and makeup for the shoot.

exile
Taylor's raw and emotional duet with Bon Iver's Justin Vernon explores the moment a former couple see each other again for the first time after their break up. We hear the pair's opposing perspectives on their relationship: Justin's character is bitter at how it seemingly ended out of the blue ("I couldn't turn things around, 'cause you never gave a warning sign"), while Taylor's character laments how many chances she gave their relationship before deciding to walk away ("I gave so many signs, so many times"). 'exile' is one of several tracks on *folklore* to use film-related metaphors to describe a relationship, a common motif in Taylor's songwriting.

my tears ricochet
Sombre chords and ethereal backing vocals give 'my tears ricochet' a fitting funeral-like atmosphere. Taylor revealed that this was the first song she wrote for *folklore*, inspired by the idea of "an embittered tormentor showing up at the funeral of his fallen object of obsession." Some fans believe the metaphorical death Taylor sings about could actually be a reference to her decision to leave Big Machine Records, with the line "And when you can't sleep at night, you hear my stolen lullabies" alluding to Taylor's dispute with Scooter Braun and Scott Borchetta over the ownership of the masters for her first six albums.

mirrorball
Taylor compares herself to the titular 'mirrorball', seen as an object to entertain others and reflect the personalities of those around her. The line "I'm still trying everything to keep you looking at me" touches on a point Taylor made in *Miss Americana* about the unreasonable expectations for women in music to reinvent themselves to stay relevant: "The female artists that I know of, they've reinvented themselves twenty times more than the male artists. They have to, or else you're out of a job! Constantly having to reinvent, constantly finding new facets of yourself that people find to be shiny..."

seven
Against a driving piano melody, Taylor reminisces about a childhood friendship with someone from a troubled home ("I think your house is haunted, your dad is always mad..."). She recalls the methods of escapism children use in difficult situations, and the naive ways her seven-year-old self tries to help ("I think you should come live with me and we can be pirates, then you won't have to cry or hide in the closet"). The line "Passed down like folk songs, our love lasts so long" is the album concept in a nutshell. As Taylor explained when she announced the album, "A tale that becomes folklore is one that is passed down and whispered around."

august
The second part of the Teenage Love Triangle, told from the perspective of the unnamed other girl who James sees behind Betty's back. She recalls their passionate affair and how it ended because James still had feelings for Betty: "So much for summer love and saying 'us', 'cause you weren't mine to lose." Although James himself dismisses it as "just a summer thing" (in 'betty'), the narrator wishes their relationship could have developed into something more, with the hypnotic refrain: "For me it was enough to live for the hope of it all, cancelled plans just in case you'd call..."

this is me trying
On the surface, this song is about someone attempting to make amends after a relationship goes wrong, accepting responsibility for their mistakes. It touches on some dark themes surrounding the narrator's mental health, including depression and alcoholism: "They told me all of my cages were mental, so I got wasted like all my potential." But the 'relationship' could also symbolise Taylor's career – in particular her return from a self-imposed hiatus in 2016-17 ("I've been having a hard time adjusting [...] didn't know if you'd care if I came back") – and her struggles with living in the public eye.

illicit affairs
This isn't the first time Taylor has sung about infidelity, but 'illicit affairs' is a far more nuanced and almost sympathetic approach to the topic than the uncompromising standpoint of 'Should've Said No' from her debut album. It is sung from the perspective of someone trapped in an affair and the endless lies it entails, as she laments her situation but feels unable to escape it. Taylor's biting delivery during the bridge perfectly captures the character's conflicting emotions: "Don't call me 'kid', don't call me 'baby'. Look at this idiotic fool that you made me."

invisible string

The title of this song is a reference to the 'red thread of fate' from East Asian mythology – the belief that soul mates are bound by an invisible red cord, and destiny will bring them together. Over the sweet melody of finger-picked guitar, Taylor sings about how all the heartbreak of past relationships ultimately led her to finding happiness with Joe Alwyn ("Hell was the journey but it brought me heaven"). Dessner explained in his interview with *Vulture* how he created the distinctive sound for what is arguably *folklore*'s most folk-like song: "It's played on this rubber bridge that my friend put on [the guitar] and it deadens the strings so that it sounds old."

mad woman

One of *folklore*'s darker tracks explores the idea that women are often unfairly dismissed as 'mad' whenever they are justifiably angry or upset. Taylor had previously spoken about this idea in a 2019 interview with *CBS News*, explaining: "A man is allowed to 'react'; a woman can only 'over-react'." Taylor's delivery is haunting, and her lyrics scathing as she takes aim at 'witch hunters' and gaslighters. Speaking to *Vulture*, Dessner said "It has a darkness that I think is cathartic... it has this very sharp tone to it, but sort of in gothic folklore. It's this record's goth song."

epiphany

'epiphany' is an ethereal ode to those on the front lines, past and present, and the idea that dreams can provide some temporary respite from the chaos. In the album announcement notes, Taylor mentions how the opening segments were inspired by her grandfather's experience serving in the Second World War, while the second verse is a reference to the medics of the Covid-19 pandemic ("Hold your hand through plastic now. 'Doc I think she's crashing out'..."). Speaking to *Vulture*, Dessner explained how he gave the song its unique sound: "It's lots of different instruments played and then slowed down and reversed. [...] it was very beautiful to get lost in."

RIGHT: Taylor pictured with her *folklore* and *evermore* collaborators, Jack Antonoff (left) and Aaron Dessner (right), at the Grammys in March 2021. With her award for *folklore*, Taylor became the first female artist to win the Album of the Year Grammy three times.

betty

There are echoes of 'Love Story' in 'betty' – a catchy melody with country motifs, a charming narrative of young romance, and a key change to make your heart soar. This is the final piece of the Teenage Love Triangle trilogy, telling events from James' perspective as he regrets his summer fling and wonders whether Betty will ever forgive him for being unfaithful. The lyrics include several callbacks to both 'cardigan' and 'august' ("Standing in your cardigan, kissing in my car again" / "She pulled up like a figment of my worst intentions [...] slept next to her, but I dreamt of you all summer long") to weave the trilogy together.

peace

While several tracks on *folklore* are sung from the perspective of fictional characters, 'peace' is one of the record's more personal songs, alluding to the impact Taylor's fame has on her relationship with Joe Alwyn. The stripped back production allows Taylor's thoughtful lyrics to shine through, as she confesses to her partner that – no matter how dedicated they are to one another – her career and celebrity status will inevitably cause complications and prevent them from having a 'normal' life together: "The devil's in the details but you got a friend in me. Would it be enough if I could never give you peace?"

hoax

The closing track is a melancholic piano ballad reflecting on a troubled relationship. The lyrics describe someone committed to her partner even though their love seems hopeless and makes her miserable: "Don't want no other shade of blue but you. No other sadness in the world would do." Dessner gave his take on the song in his interview with *Vulture*, saying, "There's sadness, but it's a kind of hopeful sadness. It's a recognition that you take on the burden of your partners, your loved ones, and their ups and downs." This feeling of 'hopeful sadness' is one that *folklore* manages to capture, and is expressed so well in many of its tracks. A perfect note for the album to end on.

"I WROTE AND RECORDED THIS IN ISOLATION, BUT GOT TO COLLABORATE WITH SOME MUSICAL HEROES OF MINE."

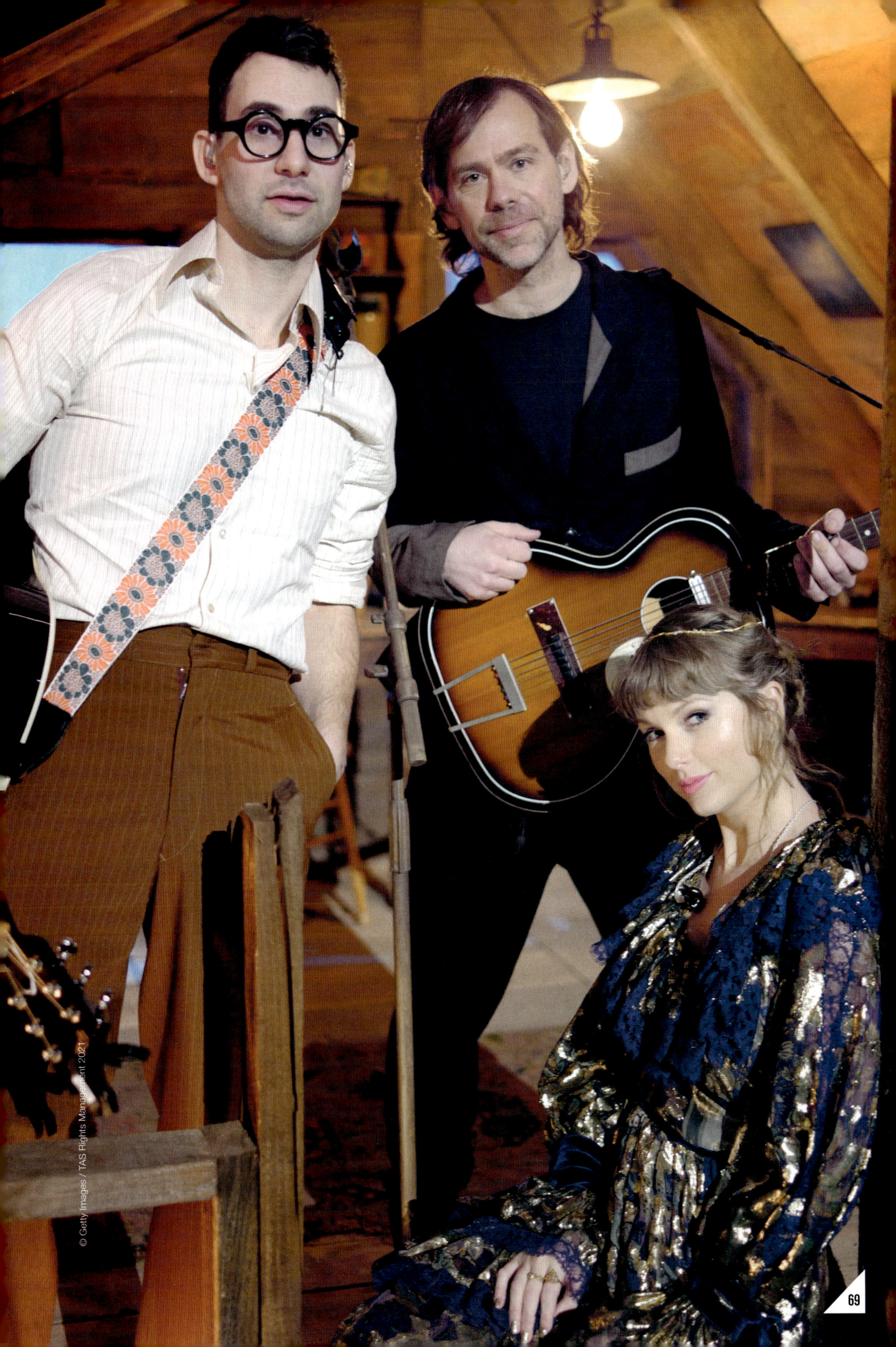

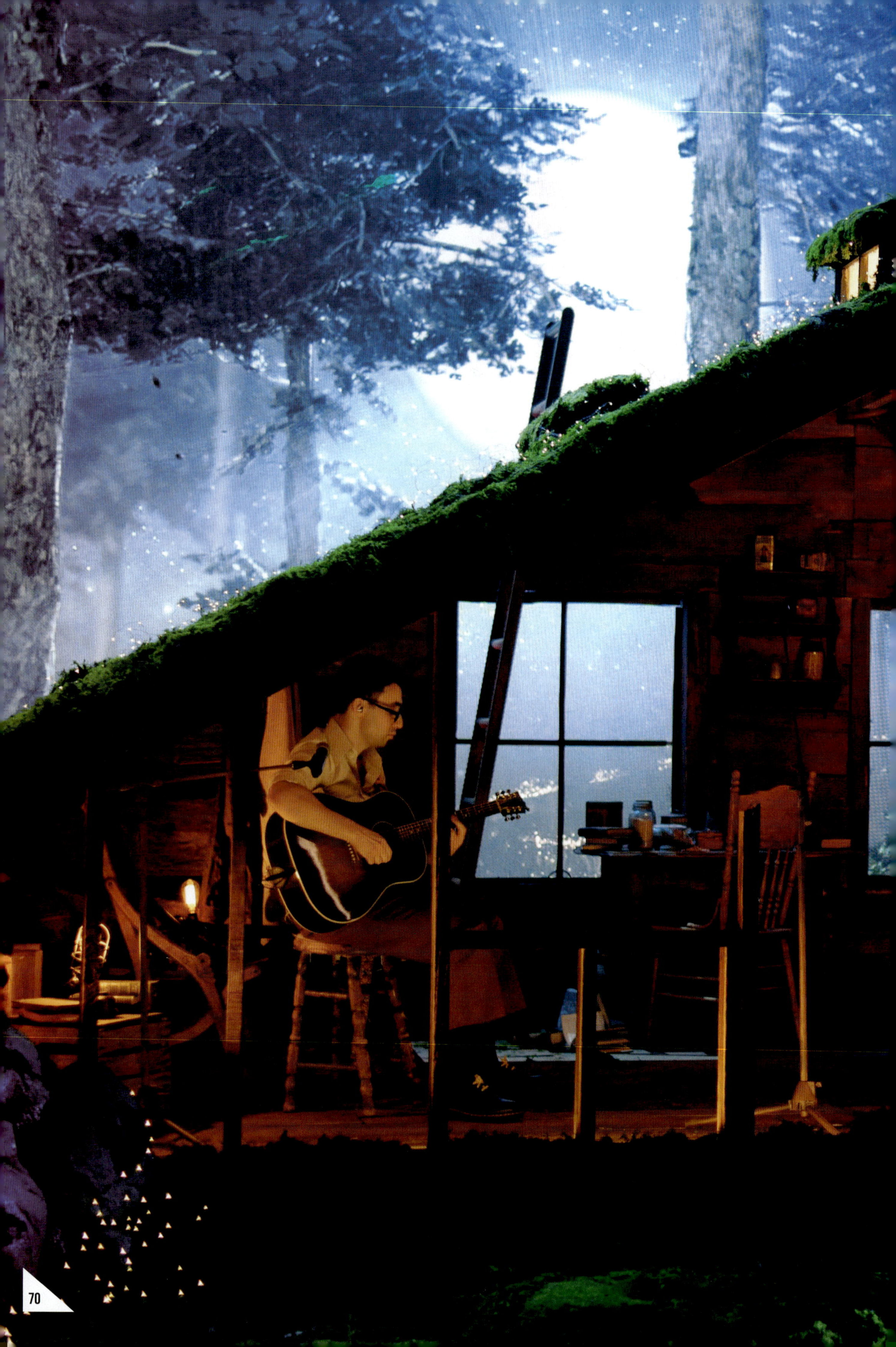

On a suitably whimsical stage set, Taylor performed a medley of tracks from *folklore* and *evermore* at the 2021 Grammys.

EVERMORE

RELEASED: DECEMBER 2020   WORDS BY: HANNAH WALES

BREAKING FROM HER TRADITION OF TREATING ALBUMS LIKE ONE-OFF ERAS, TAYLOR RELEASED **FOLKLORE**'S SISTER ALBUM JUST FIVE MONTHS LATER, WITH MORE MESMERISING STORIES

willow
Taylor picked 'willow' as the lead single from *evermore* because she liked the "witchy", "magical and mysterious" music her co-writer Aaron Dessner created and thought it set the right tone for the album. The song is about intrigue, desire, and the complexity that goes into wanting someone, with Taylor's character seemingly unsure of her crush's feelings towards her ("The more that you say, the less I know"). Taylor told fans on YouTube: "I think it sounds like casting a spell to make somebody fall in love with you."

champagne problems
This song tells the story of a man getting down on one knee to propose to his longtime college sweetheart in front of his family and friends and the woman breaking his heart by saying no. Joe Alwyn, under his alias William Bowery, created the melodic structure of the song and Taylor wrote the lyrics. Taylor told Apple Music that it was one of her favourite bridges to write because it "shifts gears" and tells the whole story, and she can't wait to perform it in front of a crowd and hear everyone sing, "She would've made such a lovely bride, what a shame she's f**ked in the head."

gold rush
In 'gold rush', the narrator is daydreaming about being in a relationship with a beautiful man everybody wants but then the dream fades as she realises "it could never be" as she wouldn't be able to handle the jealousy of being with such a heartthrob. Taylor wrote this chilled, dream-like song with Jack Antonoff, who also produced and provided background vocals, while his Bleachers bandmates played the instruments. It's one of *evermore*'s more pop-sounding tracks, with a pulsing beat and shifting tempo throughout, bookended with dreamy vocal segments.

'tis the damn season
In the notes for *evermore*, Taylor revealed that this Christmassy track is a companion piece to 'dorothea' and depicts "what happens when she comes back for the holidays and rediscovers an old flame". Dorothea suggests to her hometown ex that they briefly rekindle their old romance before she goes back to Los Angeles, with key lyrics including "I'll be yours for the weekend" and "the road not taken looks real good now". Taylor wrote the song in the middle of the night after a day of rehearsing for the *folklore: the long pond studio sessions* film at Dessner's studio and sung the lyrics to him in the kitchen the following morning.

tolerate it
Taylor continues her tradition of making track five her most vulnerable song with 'tolerate it', which is told from the perspective of a woman who loves her much older partner but he just seems ambivalent towards her. Taylor was inspired by Daphne du Maurier's novel *Rebecca*, in which the lead character is essentially ignored by her husband after they return home from their honeymoon. Taylor told Apple Music: "There was a part of me that was relating to that because at some point in my life, I felt that way."

> "I LOVED THE ESCAPISM I FOUND IN THESE IMAGINARY AND NOT IMAGINARY TALES."

no body, no crime (feat. HAIM)

Taylor was inspired by her obsession with true crime stories and wrote a murder-mystery tale that revolves around a woman named Este, who confronts her cheating husband and suddenly goes missing, and the narrator is Este's friend who avenges her murder. Taylor wrote the song solo before reaching out to one of her best friends – Este Haim – to see if her band wanted to do backing vocals. The character Este was already written in the lyrics but the real Este got to pick the reference to the restaurant chain Olive Garden. The song, which is a throwback to Taylor's country roots, marks the first collaboration between the singer and HAIM, despite them being longtime friends.

happiness

The deceptively titled 'happiness' tells the story of a woman who is adjusting to single life after "seven years in heaven" and trying to move on from the break-up and find "the new me". Despite the hurt and anger in the lyrics, it's ultimately a hopeful song, with her character singing, "There'll be happiness after you." Dessner had been working on the instrumental since 2019, thinking it would be for Big Red Machine – his experimental folk-rock band with Bon Iver's Justin Vernon – but Taylor loved the music and wrote lyrics to it. It was the last song Taylor wrote for the album, and "the new me" line also reflects the reinvention she'll undergo after this chapter.

dorothea

The companion piece to ''tis the damn season' is told from the male perspective, with Dorothea's ex wondering if she ever thinks about him back home in Tupelo after moving to Los Angeles to pursue her Hollywood dreams. The narrator is curious if she's still the same person now she's got fortune and fame and encourages her to "come back to my side". Taylor clarified in a YouTube comment that 'dorothea' doesn't continue *folklore*'s Teenage Love Triangle, but in her mind "Dorothea went to the same school as Betty, James, and Inez".

TOP: In the *evermore* liner notes, Taylor explained that she "just couldn't stop writing songs" after *folklore*, so in a career first she decided to make a sister album.

LEFT: Taylor has joked that she's the "fourth Haim sister". As well as 'no body, no crime', she has also collaborated with the trio on a remix of their song 'Gasoline'.

coney island (feat. The National)

This melancholic ballad tells the story of two exes who are sitting on a bench in Coney Island, a beachside fairground in New York, reminiscing about a past relationship and wondering where they went wrong. This marks Taylor's first collaboration with the whole of The National, not just Dessner. She originally wrote the lyrics with Alwyn and recorded it with just her voice, but they decided to get all of Dessner's bandmates involved, with lead singer Matt Berninger adding his vocals. Taylor told Apple Music she was thrilled to get her "favourite lead singer of (her) favourite band" to sing the words "happy birthday" on 'coney island', as *evermore* was released the week of her 31st birthday.

ivy

In this song, Taylor uses nature imagery to tell the story of a woman who is cheating on her husband and wondering what the husband will do if or when he finds out. Ivy is a fast-growing and notoriously hard-to-remove plant, so the metaphor implies that the narrator's secret affair is taking over, even though she knows it's a bad idea. In her message about *evermore* on social media, Taylor revealed 'ivy' was part of the "'unhappily ever after' anthology of marriages gone bad that includes infidelity, ambivalent toleration, and even murder", with the other two being 'tolerate it' and 'no body, no crime'. The song was written by Taylor, Dessner, and Antonoff, and features subtle background vocals from Vernon.

cowboy like me

This track is about two young con artists who meet while "hanging out at fancy resorts trying to score rich romantic beneficiaries", according to Taylor's album notes. They fall in love and put their old scamming lifestyles behind them ("Forever is the sweetest con"). The song features background vocals from Marcus Mumford of Mumford & Sons, who Taylor is a big fan of, and a guitar solo by Vernon.

long story short

The only uptempo pop song on *evermore* revisits themes from the *reputation* era and refers to when Taylor left the public eye in 2016 following her feud with Kanye West and his then-wife Kim Kardashian, with notable lyrics including: "And I fell from the pedestal, right down the rabbit hole, long story short, it was a bad time." Taylor "survived" that chapter and has moved on from "keeping score" and is now "all about you", presumably referring to Alwyn. She also offers up advice to her past self and tells her "not to get lost in these petty things".

marjorie
This track is about Taylor's grandmother Marjorie Finlay, an opera singer who passed away in 2003 when Taylor was 13. The song features Taylor thinking about advice she learned from her grandmother and how she regrets not fully appreciating who Finlay was because she was too young. Taylor admitted to Apple Music that she was a "wreck at times" when she wrote the song and found it hard to sing it without a catch in her throat because she was so emotional. She sent Dessner some of Finlay's opera recordings and he sampled them in the song, so Finlay is credited with background vocals. 'marjorie' is track 13 on *evermore*, while 'epiphany', which was inspired by Taylor's late grandfather, is track 13 on *folklore*.

closure
This experimental song, which has an unusual time signature, depicts the narrator receiving a letter from an estranged friend or ex who is reaching out to achieve closure and suggest they remain friends, but she isn't interested in ironing out their differences and is "fine with my spite". Vernon put Taylor's vocals through his vocal modifier to distort her sound. Dessner revealed in an interview with Billboard that Taylor originally wrote 'closure' and 'dorothea' for Big Red Machine, his band with Vernon. He explained: "The more I listened to them, not that they couldn't be Big Red Machine songs, but they felt like interesting, exciting Taylor songs."

evermore (feat. Bon Iver)
The album's title track, a piano ballad, is Taylor's second duet with Vernon after their *folklore* collaboration 'exile'. In the beginning, the narrator has "been down" for months and feels like their pain, or perhaps depression, will be "for evermore". However, it ends with the narrator feeling a glimmer of hope. Much like 'exile', Alwyn crafted the piano part and Taylor wrote the lyrics, and Vernon subsequently added the bridge, but this time around, Alwyn was able to play the piano for the recording remotely. Dessner told *Rolling Stone*: "He also wrote the piano part of 'exile,' but on the record, it's me playing it because we couldn't record him easily. But this time, we could."

TOP: Taylor continued her fruitful collaboration with Jack Antonoff (centre) and Aaron Dessner (right) to make *evermore*.

ABOVE: After plenty of fan speculation, it was confirmed that Joe Alwyn is indeed the mysterious 'William Bowery' who co-wrote several *folklore* and *evermore* tracks.

LEFT: After duetting with Taylor on 'coney island', The National's Matt Berninger (pictured) said on Twitter, "Singing a song with @taylorswift13 is like dancing with Gene Kelly."

FEARLESS (TAYLOR'S VERSION)

RELEASED: **APRIL 2021**   WORDS BY: **HANNAH WALES**

TAYLOR REVISITS HER SECOND STUDIO ALBUM, **FEARLESS**, 13 YEARS AFTER ITS ORIGINAL RELEASE TO KICKSTART HER ALBUM RE-RECORDING PROJECT

A couple of months after Scott Borchetta sold the master recordings of Taylor's first six albums – her 2006 self-titled debut through to 2017's *reputation* – to Scooter Braun, Taylor announced that she would re-record them so she could regain ownership and control of her music.

Rather than start at the beginning and re-record *Taylor Swift* first, she announced in February 2021 that she would kick off her re-recording project with *Fearless*, which scored Taylor her first Album of the Year Grammy back in 2008.

Not content with simply redoing the 13 tracks on the original album, Taylor re-recorded the 19 songs on the platinum edition of *Fearless*, 'Today was a Fairytale' from the *Valentine's Day* movie soundtrack, and six "From the Vault" tracks that "killed [her] to leave behind" when she made the album in 2008.

Taylor recruited her usual collaborators Jack Antonoff and Aaron Dessner as well as touring musicians from the *Fearless* era for the project, and she was determined to stay true to the lyrics, melodies and arrangements of the originals but improve upon their sonic quality.

"We really did go in and try to create a 'the same but better' version," she explained to PEOPLE. "I did go in line by line and listen to every single vocal… If I can improve upon it, I did. But I really did want this to be very true to what I initially thought of and what I had initially written. But better. Obviously."

This has resulted in a near replica of *Fearless* that may seem identical to the uninitiated but has subtle differences that fans who grew up with the original will notice and appreciate – for example, Taylor's vocals are stronger and more mature, the production is more polished and the quality of the recording itself has been improved.

Fans speculated that Taylor's next re-record would be *Red*, after spotting her look at the 2021 BRITs. A few months later, they were proved right…

ABOVE: Pictured with her Official Number 1 Album trophy, awarded when *Fearless (Taylor's Version)* topped the UK charts in April 2021.

RIGHT: Taylor's rather *Red*-era look at the BRIT Awards in May 2021 proved to be a hint about her next re-record project, released that November.

TAYLOR'S TRACKS 'FROM THE VAULT'

YOU ALL OVER ME
'You All Over Me' is about Taylor not being able to get over an ex following the end of a relationship, with her using similar imagery to 'Clean' from *1989*. Key lyrics include: "No amount of freedom gets you clean, I've still got you all over me." Taylor called upon country singer Maren Morris, who made a surprise appearance on the Reputation Stadium Tour, to sing background vocals on the track, and Taylor told her Instagram followers that she enjoyed being able to experiment and "include some of my favorite artists" on the final six tracks as they had never been heard before.

MR. PERFECTLY FINE
Another break-up song, 'Mr. Perfectly Fine' is widely believed to be about Joe Jonas, who Taylor dated briefly in 2008. In the track, Taylor speaks directly to a recent ex who dumped her without explanation. She seems to resent him for being "perfectly fine" after their split and moving on quickly with a new girl while she's still heartbroken. Taylor also calls the ex "casually cruel", a description also used in 'All Too Well' from *Red*. Jonas' wife, Sophie Turner, showed her support for the track on Instagram Stories, writing: "It's not NOT a bop."

WE WERE HAPPY
In this ballad, Taylor speaks to an ex and reminisces about the halcyon days of their relationship. She recruited country singer Keith Urban, whose tour she opened during her *Fearless* era, to sing harmonies on this track. Taylor wrote on Instagram about their collaborations: "I'm really honored that @keithurban is a part of this project, duetting on That's When and singing harmonies on 'We Were Happy'. I was his opening act during the *Fearless* album era and his music has inspired me endlessly."

THAT'S WHEN (feat. Keith Urban)
Her next collaboration with Urban is a duet that tells the story of a girl who leaves her boyfriend as she needs time and space "to think about all of this" and her asking when she can come back. Speaking about their collaboration on *The Ellen DeGeneres Show*, Urban revealed Taylor reached out to him about working together while he was Christmas shopping in Australia. He recalled: "I'm sitting in the food court at the shopping centre, listening to these two unreleased Taylor Swift songs. It was an unusual place to be hearing unreleased Taylor Swift music but I loved the songs and luckily got to put a vocal on both of those."

DON'T YOU
'Don't You' has a similar theme to 'Mr. Perfectly Fine' in that Taylor is still in love with an ex and he's already moved on with someone else. The exes are seeing each other in public for the first time since the split and Taylor hates that he's being so nice and friendly to her when he caused her so much heartache, and even though she doesn't hate him, she doesn't want to pretend to be friends. Taylor told Spotify that this was a "really fun song" to write with Tommy Lee James because there was "a wellspring of emotion to draw from". She also praised producer Jack Antonoff for "letting it just be really airy and sort of like a dreamscape".

BYE BYE BABY
In this track, the narrator is driving away from her former boyfriend's home after just breaking up with him. She felt so sure that they'd always have a perfect relationship but it's stopped working. Taylor wrote the song with her frequent early-day collaborator Liz Rose, who also worked on 'We Were Happy'. The demo for this track was leaked years ago, when it was originally titled 'The One Thing', but Taylor changed the title and some of the lyrics for its official release.

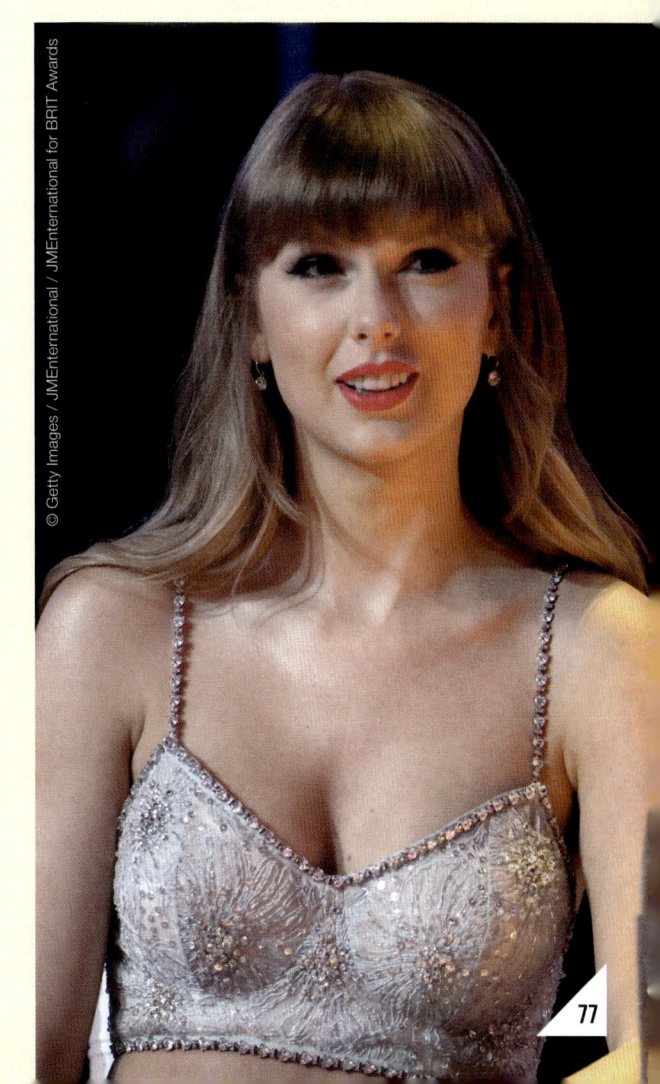

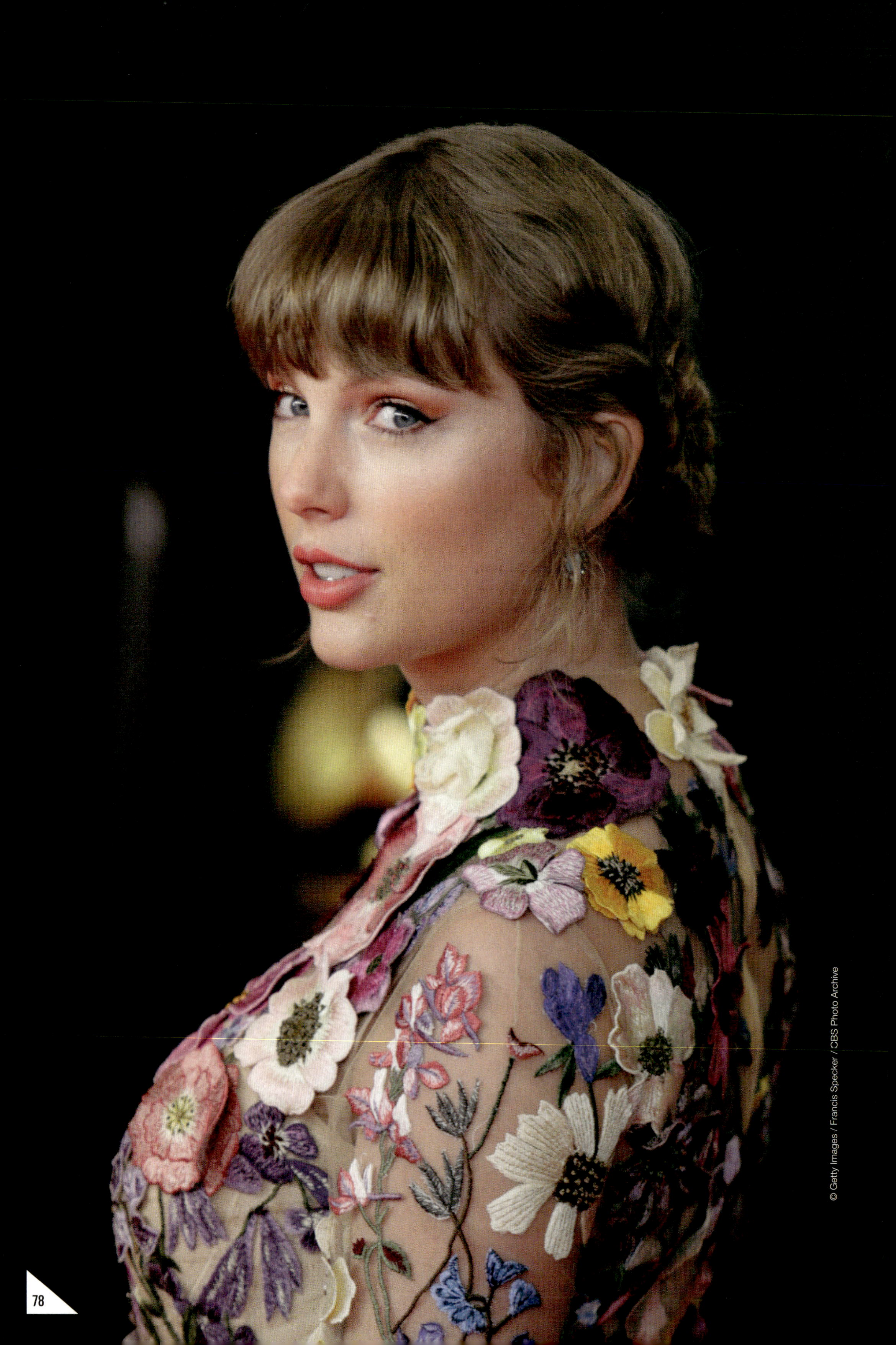

> **FEARLESS WAS AN ALBUM FULL OF MAGIC AND CURIOSITY, THE BLISS AND DEVASTATION OF YOUTH. IT WAS THE DIARY OF THE ADVENTURES AND EXPLORATIONS OF A TEENAGE GIRL WHO WAS LEARNING TINY LESSONS WITH EVERY NEW CRACK IN THE FACADE OF THE FAIRYTALE ENDING SHE'D BEEN SHOWN IN THE MOVIES.**
>
> TAYLOR SWIFT, REFLECTING ON FEARLESS BEFORE THE RELEASE OF HER RE-RECORDED VERSION IN 2021

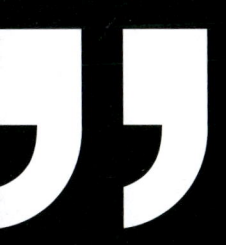

LEFT: Taylor pictured at the 63rd Annual Grammy Awards in Los Angeles, on 14 March 2021.

RED (TAYLOR'S VERSION)

RELEASED: **NOVEMBER 2021**   WORDS BY: **HANNAH WALES**

TAYLOR REVISITS HER 2012 ALBUM, **RED**, FOR THE SECOND INSTALMENT IN HER ONGOING ALBUM RE-RECORDING PROJECT

The second of Taylor's re-recorded albums, *Red (Taylor's Version)* features not only the 20 songs from the album's deluxe release, but also her 2012 charity single 'Ronan', her takes on 'Better Man' and 'Babe' (which she gave away to Little Big Town and Sugarland, respectively), and seven more 'From the Vault' tracks, including the uncut 10-minute version of 'All Too Well'.

The majority of Taylor's original collaborators returned for the project, with the exception of producers Nathan Chapman and Max Martin. Much like *Fearless (Taylor's Version)*, Taylor's vocals here are stronger and more mature and the production is sharper, but otherwise, the re-recorded tracks are very loyal to the original versions, except for 'Girl at Home', which is now more of a pop song as the acoustic guitar instrumentation has been swapped for electronic sounds.

Taylor told talk show host Seth Meyers that she was thrilled to be able to dig up old songs from the archive and give them new life with collaborators such as Phoebe Bridgers and Chris Stapleton. Explaining why the tracks were originally cut, she said, "I wanted to save them for the next album and then it turned out the next album was a whole different thing and so they got left behind."

TAYLOR'S TRACKS 'FROM THE VAULT'

BETTER MAN
This track depicts Taylor missing a relationship and her ex, even though she knows she's "better off alone." She describes the ex as a jealous person who took her for granted and sings, "We might still be in love, If you were a better man, You would've been the one, If you were a better man." After Taylor cut 'Better Man' from the original *Red* album, she gave it to country group Little Big Town, who released it in 2016. It went on to win them a Grammy Award.

NOTHING NEW (FEAT. PHOEBE BRIDGERS)
This duet addresses aging and Taylor coming to the realisation that she doesn't know as much as she thought she did at 18. The singers both wonder if the public and music industry will still want them when they're "nothing new" and a fresh and exciting ingenue comes onto the scene. Taylor explained to talk show host Seth Meyers that she wrote the song when she was 22 after she stopped feeling like "a shiny new artist." She wanted a female musician to duet with her and texted Phoebe, who replied, "I've been waiting for this text my entire life."

BABE
In this country ballad, co-written with Patrick Monahan from Train, Taylor sings to a partner who has destroyed their relationship by being unfaithful. After it didn't make it onto the original cut of *Red*, Taylor gave 'Babe' to country duo Sugarland, who released it in 2018, with her providing backing vocals and playing the 'other woman' in the music video. When the song came out, she said in an Instagram video: "I'm so happy that it gets its own life, I'm so happy that Sugarland wanted to record it, and has done such a good job with it, and I'm so stoked to be able to sing on it, too."

MESSAGE IN A BOTTLE
With this uptempo pop track, Taylor captures the anxiety and excitement that comes with meeting a new crush and wondering if they'll become something more. The song is the first track Taylor wrote with Max Martin and Shellback, her *1989* and *reputation* collaborators, and is rumoured to be about Harry Styles, due to the mention of London in the bridge.

I BET YOU THINK ABOUT ME (FEAT. CHRIS STAPLETON)
In this country-leaning song, Taylor sings about a relationship ending because her boyfriend felt their upbringings were "too different." She feels certain that he thinks of her despite being with someone else, singing, "When you realised I'm harder to forget than I was to leave, And I bet you think about me." Fans have speculated that the track is about her ex-boyfriend Jake Gyllenhaal because the song mentions the partner growing up in "glamorous, shiny, bright Beverly Hills." Taylor wrote the track in June 2011 with Lori McKenna and they wanted to "make people laugh with it." She told a country radio station, "We wanted this song to be like a comedic, tongue-in-cheek, funny, not caring what anyone thinks about you sort of break-up song." The accompanying music video stars Miles Teller as Taylor's ex.

FOREVER WINTER
In this track, which Taylor co-wrote with Mark Foster from Foster the People, the pop star is constantly worrying and stressing about her partner's wellbeing as he seems to be struggling with his mental health. Key lyrics include, "I pull at every thread trying to solve the puzzles in his head," and, "If I was standing there in your apartment, I'd take that bomb in your head and disarm it."

RUN (FEAT. ED SHEERAN)
In her second duet with Ed Sheeran on the album, they sing about getting out of town and going where "no one else is." It is the first song they ever wrote together and 'Everything Has Changed' – an original *Red* track – followed around a week later. Ed told Capital FM that 'Run' was his favourite of the two and he always hoped it would resurface. He said, "I've never really wanted to nudge Taylor about it, because it's her song and her thing. But I've always been secretly hoping that one day she'd be like, 'Hey, this one was cool'. And so, we recorded that… I'm so happy it's seeing the light of day."

THE VERY FIRST NIGHT
In this dance-pop track, Taylor reminisces fondly about a past relationship and wishes she could go "back in time" to the night they met as she misses him so much. Taylor wrote this song with Espen Lind and Amund Bjørklund of Norwegian songwriting and production duo Espionage.

ALL TOO WELL (10 MINUTE VERSION)
The crown jewel of the *Red* re-release is the extended version of this fan-favourite ballad, which features more verses and a long outro. The song is widely accepted to be about Gyllenhaal, and the new lyrics seemingly hint that he cited their nine-year age gap as the reason to break up. Taylor told talk show host Jimmy Fallon that she was excited for her fans to hear the original lyrics, which she wrote when she was 21 before cutting them down to a normal song length. She said she turned up "really sad and upset" to rehearsals one day and "started ad-libbing what I was going through, and what I was feeling, and it went on, and the song kept building and building and building in intensity, and the song just went on for about 10 to 15 minutes of us doing this." She believes this version will become the definitive version of the song. Taylor also wrote and directed the *All Too Well* short film starring Sadie Sink and Dylan O'Brien.

LEFT: Taylor performing at the Rock & Roll Hall of Fame induction ceremony in October 2021, where she inducted Carole King.

TOP RIGHT: Taylor wrote and directed a short film, *All Too Well* – based on the 10-minute version of the track – starring Dylan O'Brien and Sadie Sink (pictured).

MIDNIGHTS

RELEASED: OCTOBER 2022

RETURNING TO POP AFTER A TWO-ALBUM FOLK DETOUR, TAYLOR MADE A CONCEPT RECORD INSPIRED "BY THE STORIES OF 13 SLEEPLESS NIGHTS"

LAVENDER HAZE

Taylor first heard the common 1950s phrase "Lavender Haze" while watching *Mad Men* and discovered it meant being in an "all-encompassing love glow". She sings about doing everything she can to stay in the lavender haze, such as ignoring outside opinions and tabloid gossip. Taylor seemingly also addresses the frequent speculation that she was engaged to her then boyfriend Joe Alwyn by singing, "All they keep asking me is if I'm gonna be your bride". The lyrics are reminiscent of 'Delicate' as Taylor praises Alwyn for handling the scrutiny she had been under at the start of their relationship so "beautifully". Taylor's good friend, actress Zoë Kravitz, served as a co-writer on the song and provided backing vocals.

MAROON

A call-back to the title of her 2012 album and song 'Red', 'Maroon' sees Taylor reminiscing about the highs and lows of a failed relationship and admitting she still thinks about it every day. In the bridge, she sings, "And I wake with your memory over me / That's a real lasting legacy to leave." Maroon and burgundy are darker than the "burning red" in 'Red' and suggest a more mature love.

ANTI-HERO

In the album's chart-topping lead single, Taylor gets super candid about her insecurities. Taylor explained on social media that it is one of her favourite songs because it's "really honest" about her self-criticism. She said, "I really don't think I've delved this far into my insecurities in this much detail before". She described the track as a "guided tour" of the things she hates about herself and admitted she struggles with not feeling like a real person and the idea that her life has become "unmanageably sized". You can draw parallels between 'Anti-Hero' and 'The Archer', from the album *Lover*, because they both feature confessional lyrics about self-loathing.

LEFT: Taylor wrote and produced *Midnights* alongside her long-time collaborator, Jack Antonoff

RIGHT: Taylor announced her new album at the 2022 MTV Video Music Awards

SNOW ON THE BEACH (feat. Lana Del Rey)
This dreamy pop ballad features backing vocals from Lana Del Rey. Taylor told her fans that she will be "grateful for life" that Del Rey agreed to appear on the song as she considers her "one of the best musical artists ever". The song is about the surreal moment where two people fall in love with each other at the exact same time. The song, which also name-drops Janet Jackson and her 2001 song 'All For You', features drums by *All Too Well: The Short Film* star Dylan O'Brien, as Taylor and her collaborator Jack Antonoff suggested the actor record the drum track when they were hanging out drinking wine in Jack's home studio.

YOU'RE ON YOUR OWN, KID
Taylor's fifth track starts with a recollection of an early hometown relationship before morphing into a tale about the beginnings of her career and her struggles during her rise to fame. Taylor candidly references her past eating disorder by singing, "(I) starved my body" in the bridge. She admits she burned some bridges to get ahead with the lyrics, "'Cause there were pages turned with the bridges burned / Everything you lose is a step you take." The track begins with a pulsing beat and builds into an eventual crescendo.

MIDNIGHT RAIN
Accompanied by a minimalist drum beat and synth sounds, Taylor reflects on a past relationship that ended because she wanted to pursue her career instead of settling down. She recalls how they were the opposites of each other, with him being the "sunshine" and her "midnight rain", and how they wanted different things out of the relationship. He "wanted a bride" but she was busy "chasing that fame" and making a name for herself in music, and she changed a lot while he stayed the same.

QUESTION...?
In the seventh track, Taylor asks her ex a series of questions about their time together and wonders if every relationship he's been in since has felt like "second best after that meteor strike". She asks if he regrets not putting up more of a fight at the end of their romance and if he wishes he could still touch her. O'Brien, Antonoff, his sister Rachel and Taylor's brother Austin provided crowd noises for the song, which begins with an interpolation of Taylor's 2016 single 'Out of the Woods', which is also about a failed relationship.

VIGILANTE SHIT
This trap-oriented track tells the story of a woman on a quest for revenge after a man does her wrong. She also helps other scorned women "get even" with liars and cheats, singing, "She needed cold, hard proof, so I gave her some (...) Now she gets the house, gets the kids, gets the pride." The song could have easily fit in with the dark revenge theme of *reputation*, while it also parallels the vigilante story Taylor tells in 'no body, no crime' from *evermore*. This is the only song on the standard album that Taylor wrote by herself.

BEJEWELED
In this bubblegum pop song, Taylor expresses her frustrations with a lover who has been "walkin' all over my peace of mind" and not treating her the way she deserves. Knowing her self-worth, she goes on a night out to regain her confidence and prove she's still got what it takes to "make the whole place shimmer". She admitted to iHeartRadio that the song is also her way of "hyping myself up to return to pop music" and checking to see if she is still bejewelled enough for pop after her folk albums.

LABYRINTH

Taylor sings about entering into a new relationship with some hesitancy in this hazy dreamscape. With her breathy, ethereal vocals, she reveals she was still hurting from a past break-up when she met her new lover. She thought she would be "gettin' over (the ex) my whole life" but she bounces back and finds herself falling in love again, with her singing, "I thought the plane was goin' down / How'd you turn it right around?"

KARMA

Returning to her recurring theme of karma, Taylor reflects on how karma has served her well as she is happy with her life and wonders if her detractors can say the same. She told iHeartRadio that 'Karma' "is written from a perspective of feeling really happy, really proud of the way your life is, feeling like this must be a reward for doing stuff right". Taylor has explored the concept of karma throughout her discography, such as 'Look What You Made Me Do', and in relation to her past feuds with Kanye West, Kim Kardashian and Scooter Braun. Fans once speculated that Taylor had made an album called Karma after the words appeared in the music video for 'The Man' in early 2020 but this never materialised.

SWEET NOTHING

Taylor wrote this dreamy pop ballad with Alwyn under his William Bowery pseudonym following their collaborations on *folklore* and *evermore*. The track reflects on how simple, easy and calm their relationship is at home in contrast to their hectic public lives. She finds peace knowing that Alwyn wants "sweet nothing" from her while she faces pressure and high expectations from the outside world. The title has a double meaning, as "sweet nothings" also describes words of affection exchanged between lovers. In the opening verse, Taylor references collecting a pebble from a shore in County Wicklow in Ireland, where Alwyn filmed his 2022 TV show, *Conversations with Friends*.

TOP RIGHT: Taylor's friend, actress Zoë Kravitz, co-wrote 'Lavender Haze' and provided backing vocals

RIGHT: Singer Lana Del Rey provided vocals for and co-wrote the song 'Snow On The Beach'

MASTERMIND

In the standard album's closing track, Taylor confesses that it was not fate that brought her and a lover together – it was actually her calculated scheming. The lyrics contrast the theme of destiny in love illustrated in previous songs such as 'invisible string'. In the standout confessional moment in the track, Taylor sings, "No one wanted to play with me as a little kid / So I've been scheming like a criminal ever since." She told iHeartRadio that the song is the "romantic version" of her Easter egg-dropping strategy. She explained, "You have been planning and plotting things and making them look like an accident — and I think that's sort of an inside joke between me and my fans, that I tend to do that".

"TAYLOR REFLECTS ON HOW KARMA HAS SERVED HER WELL AS SHE IS HAPPY WITH HER LIFE."

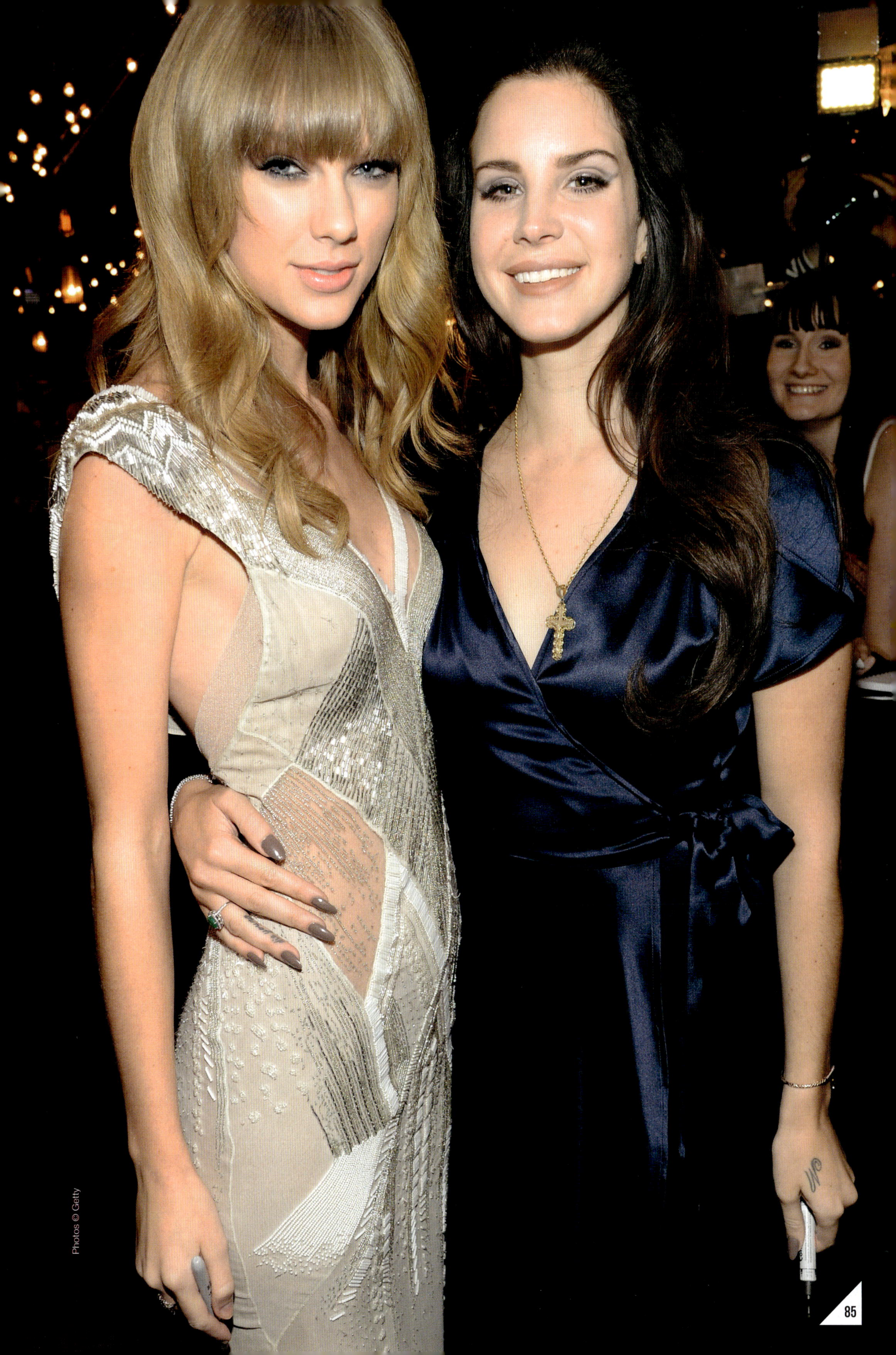

Photos © Getty

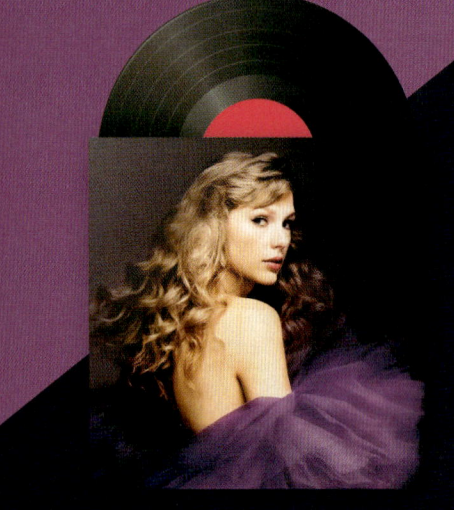

SPEAK NOW (TAYLOR'S VERSION)

RELEASED: JULY 2023   WORDS BY: JESSICA LEGGETT

REVISITING HER THIRD STUDIO ALBUM, TAYLOR IS OFFICIALLY HALFWAY THROUGH HER MISSION TO RE-RECORD HER FIRST SIX STUDIO ALBUMS

A country-pop album that also embraces a pop-rock sound, *Speak Now* was written solely by Taylor – a response to the critics who had claimed that she did not write her own songs. Announcing the release of *Speak Now (Taylor's Version)* on Twitter, Taylor explained that "the songs that came from this time in my life were marked by their brutal honesty, unfiltered diaristic confessions and wild wistfulness. I love this album because it tells a tale of growing up, flailing, flying and crashing... and living to speak about it."

Alongside the 14 songs from the standard edition of *Speak Now* and two tracks – 'Ours' and 'Superman' – from the deluxe edition, Taylor has added six 'From the Vault' tracks to the album. These new additions include collaborations with Fall Out Boy and Paramore's Hayley Williams, who both inspired the original record. While the re-recorded original songs were produced with Christopher Rowe (who also worked with Taylor on the re-recordings of *Fearless* and *Red*), she reunited with longtime collaborators Jack Antonoff and Aaron Dessner to produce the six bonus songs.

As with the other *Taylor's Versions*, her vocals are more mature and polished, which is hardly a surprise considering the original *Speak Now* was released in 2010. While most songs vary ever so slightly in length compared to the originals, the most notable difference in this re-recording is the lyric change in 'Better Than Revenge'. Taylor has changed the controversial line "She's better known for the things that she does on the mattress" to "He was a moth to the flame, she was holding the matches."

TAYLOR'S TRACKS 'FROM THE VAULT'

ELECTRIC TOUCH (FEAT. FALL OUT BOY)
The first of two collaborations on the album, this pop-punk track with a cinematic production sees Swift and Patrick Stump, lead singer of Fall Out Boy, explore the uncertainty and giddiness ahead of a first date, as well as the hope of new love after experiencing heartbreak, "All I know is this could either break my heart or bring it back to life." This song is not the first time that Swift and Fall Out Boy have joined forces, as they previously performed together during the 2013 Victoria's Secret Fashion Show, and Stump made a special guest appearance during Taylor's Red Tour. Eager Swifties will have also noticed the timestamp "8:05" in the lyrics, which adds up to 13, Taylor's lucky number.

WHEN EMMA FALLS IN LOVE
This sweet and poignant song was co-produced with Dessner and follows the journey of Emma, a captivating young woman who falls in and out of love, ultimately finding her true love in the end. Swaying between a ballad with a piano melody to a country-pop song backed by guitars, the song expresses Taylor's admiration for her friend and is complimented by her heartfelt vocals. After the album's release, Taylor revealed during her first show in Kansas City for the Eras Tour that this song was written about one of her best friends, further fuelling existing speculation that the 'Emma' in question is her close friend, actress Emma Stone.

TOP RIGHT: Taylor performs *Speak Now*'s 'Enchanted' during the Eras Tour in a stunning fairytale ballgown.

RIGHT: Taylor posing with Hayley Williams from Paramore back in 2010. The pair have been friends for many years.

"TAYLOR'S VOCALS ARE MORE MATURE AND POLISHED."

I CAN SEE YOU

A sultry and sexy tune that is filled with flirtatious innuendos, 'I Can See You' sees Taylor addressing a possible lover and their attraction to one another. Co-produced with Antonoff, the song features a guitar riff that gives it an edgier element in comparison to the rest of the album, and overall boasts an experimental sound reminiscent of that explored by Taylor in the albums *reputation* and *Midnights*, while the sexually suggestive lyrics are a reminder of the song 'Dress.' This is currently the only vault track from the album to get a proper music video, which stars Taylor's ex-boyfriend, Taylor Lautner.

CASTLES CRUMBLING
(FEAT. HAYLEY WILLIAMS)

This is arguably one of the most emotional and introspective songs on the album. 'Castles Crumbling' sees Taylor teaming up with Hayley Williams, a long-time friend and lead vocalist of Paramore. In an interview with *Coup de Main* magazine, Hayley explained that the song is "about an experience that both of us have shared growing up in the public eye." Indeed, the lyrics explore the complexities and pressures of fame, self-doubt and ultimately, Taylor's fear of losing the support of her fans and her career. Another Antonoff co-production, 'Castles Crumbling' is a moody ballad that stands out from the majority of the album, which largely focuses on romantic relationships.

FOOLISH ONE

In this track, co-produced with Dessner, Taylor narrates the pain of unrequited love, the hopeless romantic inside her waiting in vain for the person she loves to return her feelings. The song's melancholic production emphasises the heartbreak of teen love and inexperience, but ultimately ends with Taylor accepting that the person she loves has chosen someone else and realising her foolishness. Since the song's release, it has been heavily speculated that 'Foolish One' is about Taylor's ex, singer John Mayer, although this has not been confirmed. Interestingly, the line "It's delicate" in the second verse ended up becoming an entire song for her 2017 album *reputation*.

TIMELESS

The closing track on *Speak Now (Taylor's Version)* is a sentimental ballad that explores the idea of fate and enduring love. In the lyrics, Taylor imagines her relationship in different time periods and decides that no matter what, they would have found each other: "Even if we'd met on a crowded street in 1944, you still would've been mine." A country-pop classic that fits in well with the original songs of *Speak Now*, 'Timeless' is backed by a mixture of acoustic guitars, drums, and piano, and even includes a reference to Romeo & Juliet, the inspiration for her hit song 'Love Story'. In a sweet and nostalgic nod, the lyric video for 'Timeless' includes photos of Taylor's grandparents, Majorie and Robert Finlay, whose relationship likely inspired the song.

CHAPTER 3

TEAM TAYLOR

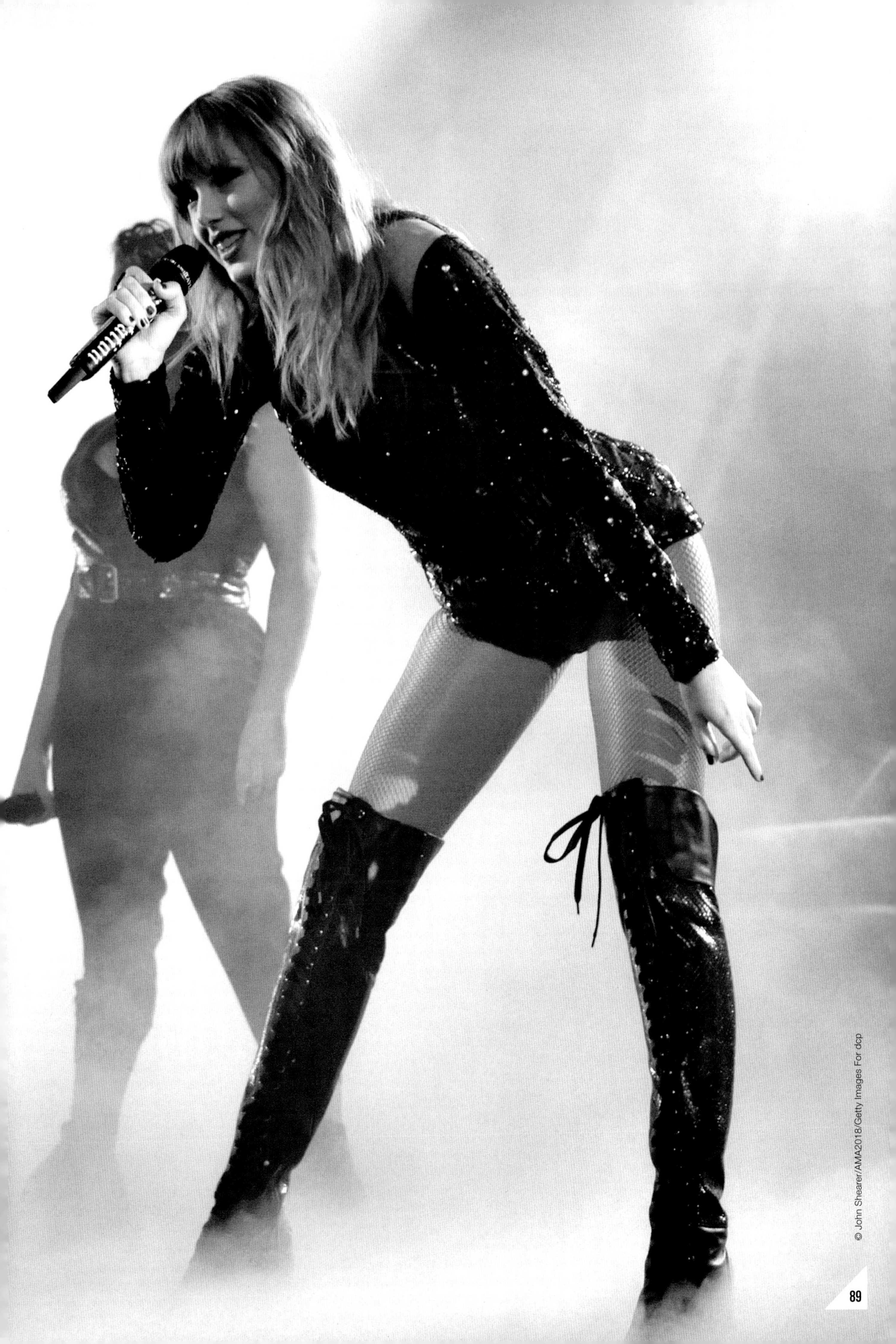

© John Shearer/AMA2018/Getty Images For dcp

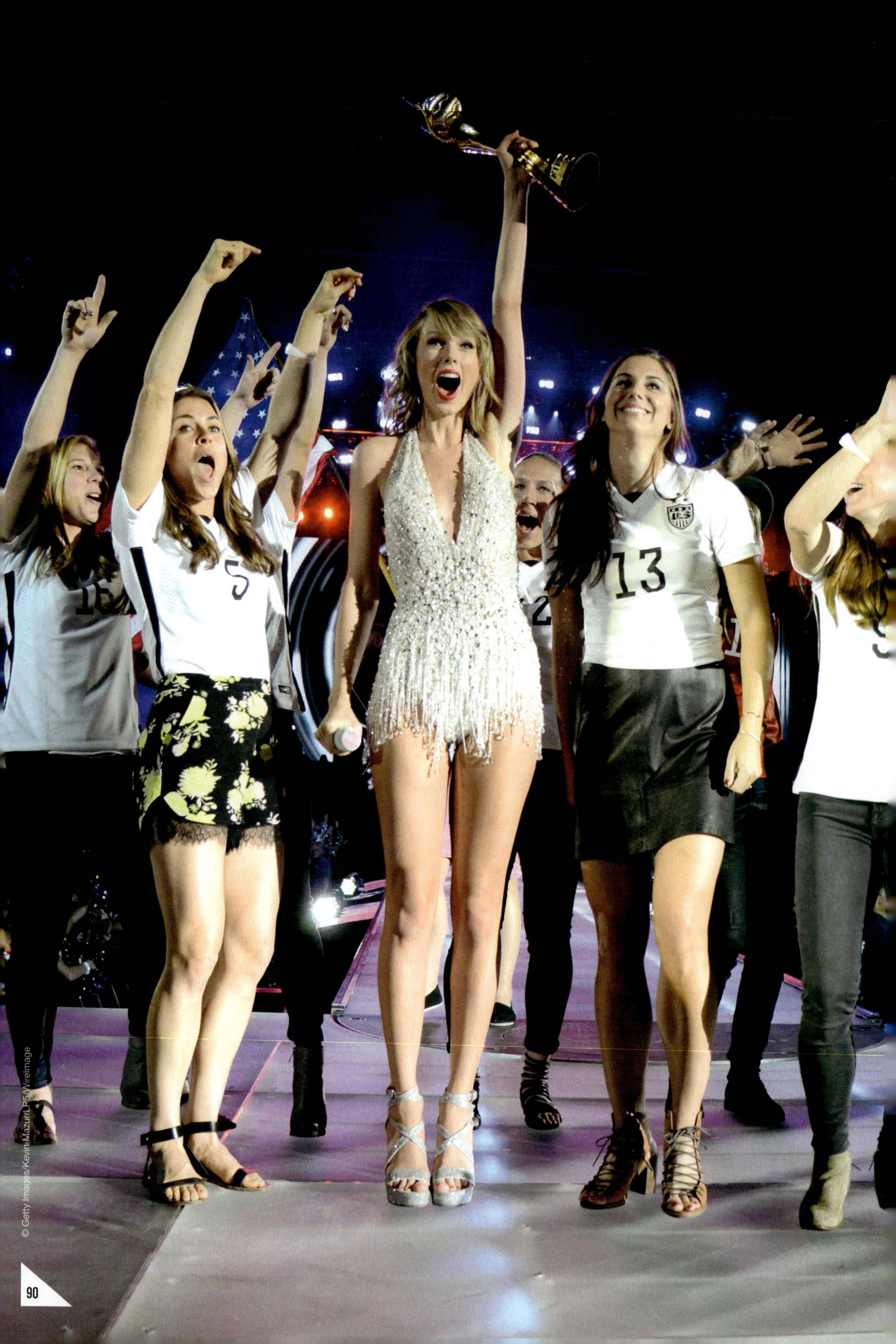

TEAM TAYLOR

FROM HER HIGH-PROFILE ROMANCES TO HER FAMOUS FRIENDSHIPS AND CELEBRITY FALL OUTS, TAYLOR WOULDN'T BE THE STAR SHE IS WITHOUT THE RICH NETWORK OF RELATIONSHIPS THAT SURROUND HER. TAKE A DEEP DIVE INTO WHO'S ON 'TEAM TAYLOR' — AND WHO ISN'T...

WORDS BY RACHEL FINN

TAYLOR'S RELATIONSHIPS

Taylor's dating life has been a central focus of her career, with her honest and raw look at teenage romance being one of the things that drew so many fans to her when she started releasing music. But, as the saying goes, the course of true love never did run smooth, and Taylor had her fair share of ups and downs.

Around the start of the Eras Tour in spring 2023, rumours began to swirl that Taylor had ended her relationship with British actor Joe Alwyn, who she had been seeing since 2016. Throughout their relationship, Taylor and Joe had kept many details of their relationship under wraps, and the end of it was no different – neither have directly confirmed, let alone commented on, the break up itself. More recently, fans and the media were convinced Taylor had briefly been seeing The 1975's Matty Healy. The pair were spotted out and about together following Taylor's break up with Joe. Again, these rumours have not been officially confirmed or denied.

While they are no longer a couple, Joe has been a huge part of Taylor's life. It's likely he and Taylor met at an entertainment industry event. Some fans think 'Dress', from Taylor's 2017 album *reputation* might hold some clues. The lyric in question? "Flashback to when you met me, your buzzcut and my hair bleached." Taylor bleached her hair

LEFT: Taylor was joined on stage by members of the US Women's Soccer team during The 1989 World Tour back in July 2015.

ABOVE: Joe Alwyn appeared in films such as *Billy Lynn's Long Half-Time Walk*, *The Favourite* and TV drama *Conversations with Friends*.

a striking platinum blonde for the 2016 Met Gala and Joe, you guessed it, turned up to the ceremony with his usually mid-length hair in a soldier-short buzzcut, leading some fans to believe that might be where the couple first met.

At the time, Taylor was in a relationship with Scottish DJ Calvin Harris, though they reportedly broke up not long after the Gala. After her subsequent relationship with actor Tom Hiddleston came to an end in September 2016, rumours that Joe and Taylor had become an item began to circulate in the media.

Taylor and Joe didn't confirm their relationship for months, but they were occasionally spotted at the same events, even if not pictured together. The pair were reportedly at the same Kings of Leon concert after-party in October 2016 and then, a month later, Taylor was seen sneaking into the premiere of Joe's film *Billy Lynn's Long Halftime Walk*. But it wasn't until the couple were photographed having coffee together in Nashville the following June that their relationship seemed to be confirmed.

Taylor had good reason to want to try and keep her growing relationship with Joe on the down-low. Famous from a young age, she'd had to contend with having all of her relationships dissected by fans and the media alike. After breaking up with Calvin Harris, she quickly found herself dating Tom Hiddleston just weeks later, something that the public and press leapt on with arguably unfair scrutiny. With Joe, Taylor seemed keen to keep her private life, well, private.

Speaking to *The Guardian* before the release of her seventh album, *Lover*, Taylor spoke about why keeping her relationship with Joe quiet was so important to her. "I've learned that if I do [speak about it], people think it's up for discussion, and our relationship isn't up for discussion," she explained. "If you and I were having a glass of wine right now, we'd be talking about it – but it's just that it goes out into the world. That's where the boundary is, and that's where my life has become manageable. I really want to keep it feeling manageable."

Joe had also spoken, if only briefly, about how much he valued the private side of their relationship. In an interview with *Esquire* from 2018, he was asked if he sought out any guidance from friends when the two of them first started dating. "I didn't seek out advice on that," he replied. "Because I know what I feel about it. I think there's a very clear line as to what somebody should share, or feel like they have to share, and what they don't want to and shouldn't have to."

The pair also worked together on Taylor's 2020 records, *folklore* and *evermore*, as Joe co-wrote and

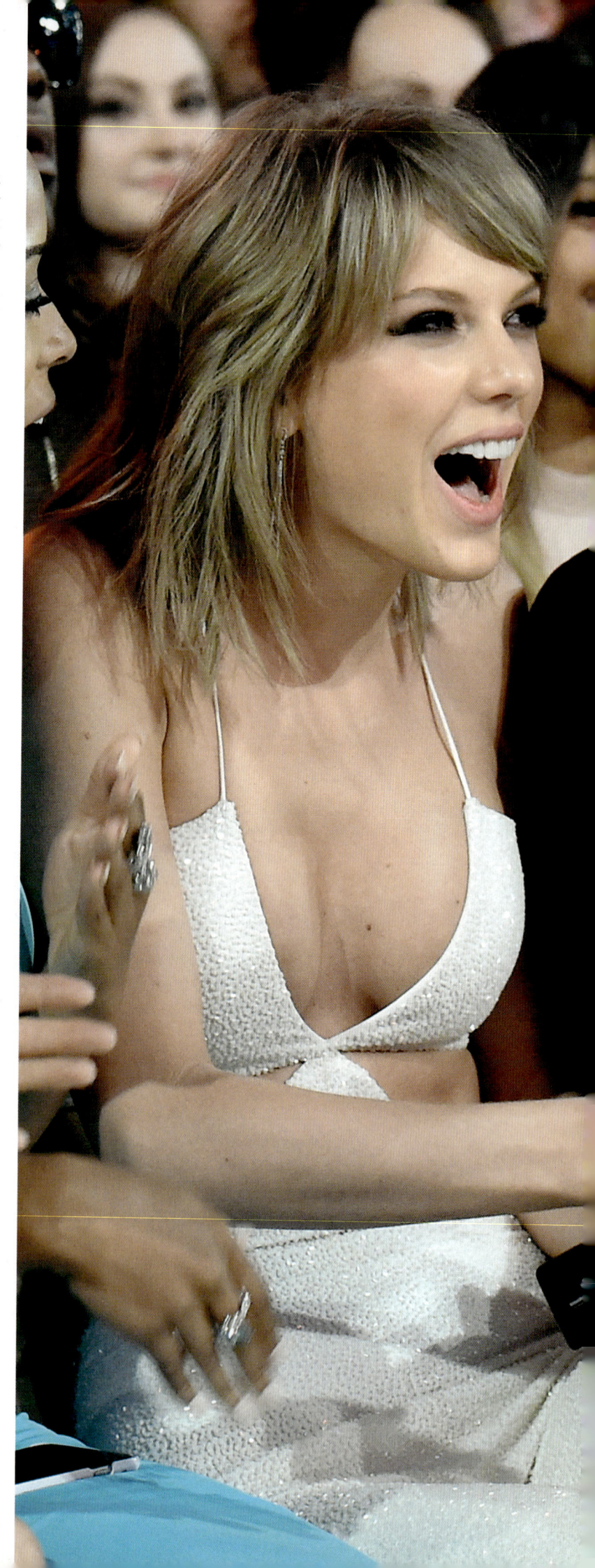

LEFT: Taylor dated DJ Calvin Harris for just over a year between 2015 and 2016.

co-produced several songs for the albums under the pseudonym William Bowery. In a rare public mention of their relationship, when folklore won the Album of the Year Grammy in 2021, Taylor thanked Joe in her acceptance speech: "[I want to thank] Joe, who is the first person that I play every single song that I write, and I had the best time writing songs with you in quarantine"

Before Joe, Taylor's approach to her romantic relationships had been quite different and, as well as singing about her exes in her music, she often spoke publicly about them too. Taylor dated Joe Jonas of the Jonas Brothers between July and October 2008, with things ending when Joe broke up with Taylor via a phone call. "When I find that person that is right for me [...] I'm not even going to be able to remember the boy who broke up with me over the phone in 25 seconds when I was 18," she said on The Ellen DeGeneres Show after the break up, explaining that the song 'Forever & Always' is about their relationship.

Taylor's 2012 single 'We Are Never Ever Getting Back Together' is rumoured to be about her relationship with actor Jake Gyllenhaal, who she dated between October and December 2010. She calls him out in the song for his 'exhausting' change of heart and musical taste, joking: "You hide away and find your peace of mind with some indie record that's much cooler than mine." She told Rolling Stone in 2014 that her song 'Out of the Woods' – rumoured to be about Harry Styles, who she dated from late 2012 until early 2013 – is about a relationship where "Every day was a struggle. Forget making plans for life – we were just trying to make it to next week."

When Taylor and Calvin Harris broke up after a 15-month relationship in June 2016, it seemed she was more than ready to make her future relationships more private. "I went out on a normal amount of dates in my early 20s, and I got absolutely slaughtered for it," she told Vogue. "It took a lot of hard work and altering my decision making. I didn't date for two and a half years [before Calvin]. Should I have had to do that? No." She has often criticised the fact that her relationships were often reduced to simply being fodder for internet slideshows.

Though Taylor hasn't spoken much publicly about her any plans to settle down, she did talk about potential future family plans in her 2019 Netflix documentary Miss Americana. "There's a part of me that feels like I'm 57 years old," she said, "But then there's a part of me that's like definitely not ready to have kids, definitely not ready for all this grown-up stuff. I kind of don't really have the luxury of figuring stuff out because my life is planned two years ahead of time."

For now, Taylor seems happy with being single again, indirectly confirming her recent splits on social media. Alongside photos of her 2023 Fourth of July party – with guests including some famous single BFFs like Selena Gomez and the Haim sisters – Taylor wrote, "Happy belated Independence Day from your local neighborhood independent girlies".

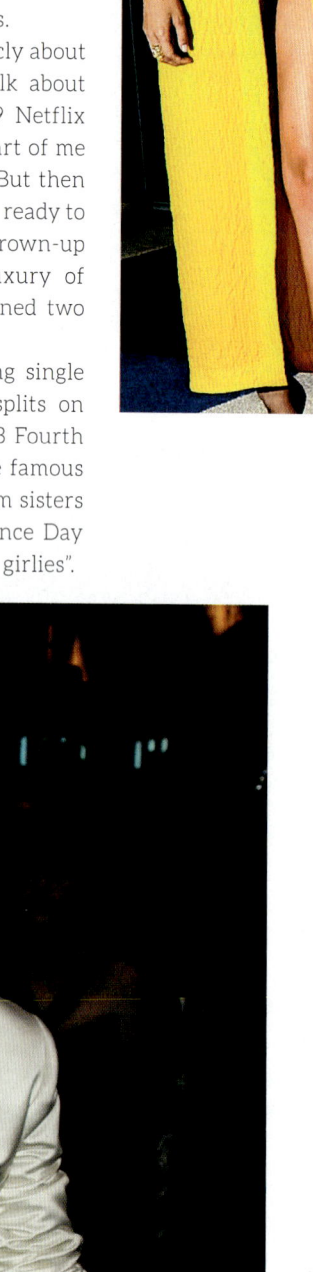

TAYLOR'S 'SQUAD'

It's not just Taylor's past romances that have drawn attention, but her friendship group too. Taylor moved away from her country music roots and became a bona fide pop artist with the 2014 release of her fifth studio album *1989* and with that as well came the emergence of Taylor's 'girl squad', a group of famous musicians, actresses and models who were regularly seen with Taylor at parties, industry events and celebrating the Fourth of July during Taylor's extravagant yearly bashes at her Rhode Island mansion.

Taylor counted the likes of actors Lena Dunham, Emma Stone and Hailee Steinfeld, models Karlie Kloss, Cara Delevigne and Gigi Hadid, and fellow pop stars Lorde, Haim and Hayley Williams of Paramore as part of her 'squad', among others. They were regularly seen hanging out on each other's Instagram feed, with many of them also starring as members of Taylor's all-female fighting force in the music video for her song 'Bad Blood' and appearing on stage during shows for her 1989 World Tour.

Speaking about why she wanted to showcase her new friendship group to the world during her *1989*-era, she said it came down to the insecurities she had over not having had many friends growing up.

ABOVE: Matty Healy's appearance at some shows of the Eras Tour in 2023 helped to fuel the rumours he and Taylor were dating.

TOP: Some members of Taylor's squad assemble at the 2015 MTV VMAs. From left to right: Gigi Hadid, Martha Hunt, Hailee Steinfeld, Cara Delevingne, Selena Gomez, Taylor Swift, Serayah, Mariska Hargitay, Lily Aldridge and Karlie Kloss.

LEFT: Taylor with Joe Jonas at the 2008 MTV Video Music Awards.

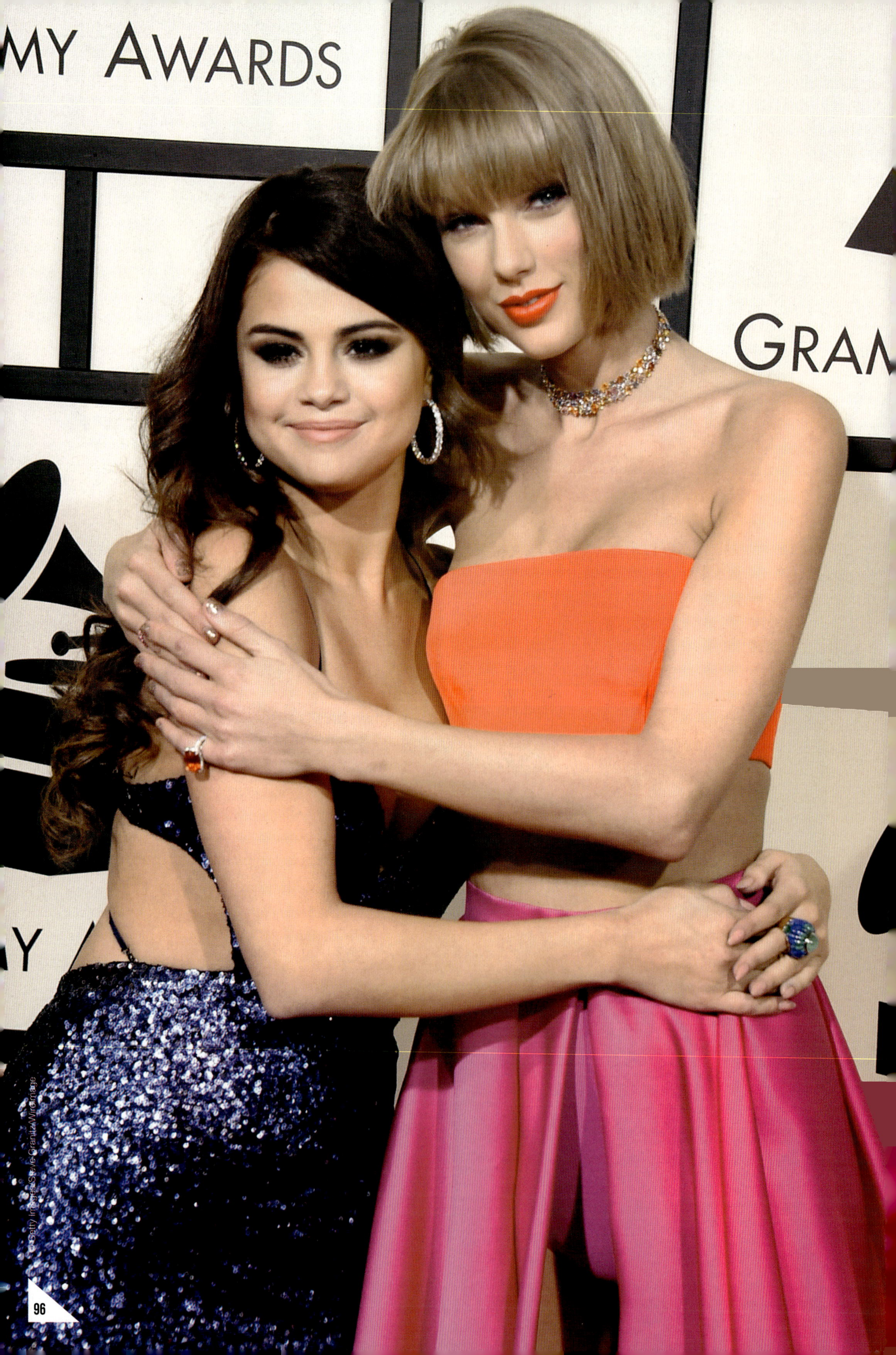
MY AWARDS
GRAM

" SHE HAS SHOWED UP FOR ME IN WAYS THAT I WOULD HAVE NEVER EXPECTED. FLOWN IN BECAUSE I WAS HURT AND WAS GOING THROUGH SOMETHING. STUFF THAT WAS GOING ON WITH MY FAMILY. IT'S BEEN PROVEN YEAR AFTER YEAR AND IN EVERY MOMENT OF MY LIFE THAT SHE IS ONE OF MY BEST FRIENDS IN THE WORLD. WE DON'T AGREE ON EVERYTHING, BUT WE RESPECT EACH OTHER WITH EVERYTHING. "

SELENA GOMEZ ON HER FRIENDSHIP WITH TAYLOR

LEFT: Selena Gomez and Taylor have been friends for over a decade, supporting each other's careers along the way.

"CONSTANTLY BEING IN THE SPOTLIGHT MEANS TAYLOR'S DISAGREEMENTS AND FEUDS ARE OFTEN BRUTALLY PUBLIC."

"Even as an adult, I still have recurring flashbacks of sitting at lunch tables alone or hiding in a bathroom stall, or trying to make a new friend and being laughed at," she wrote in an essay for *Elle* in 2019.

"In my twenties I found myself surrounded by girls who wanted to be my friend. So I shouted it from the rooftops, posted pictures, and celebrated my newfound acceptance into a sisterhood, without realizing that other people might still feel the way I did when I felt so alone. It's important to address our long-standing issues before we turn into the living embodiment of them."

Over time, the social media posts celebrating Taylor's sisterhood died down and, although many of them still remain close, other members of Taylor's 'squad' seemed to drift apart. She addressed this in the same essay for *Elle*, writing about how friendships can shift over time: "Something about 'we're in our young twenties!' hurls people together into groups that can feel like your chosen family. And maybe they will be for the rest of your life. Or maybe they'll just be your comrades for an important phase, but not forever. It's sad but sometimes when you grow, you outgrow relationships. You may leave behind friendships along the way, but you'll always keep the memories."

TAYLOR VS THE WORLD

Constantly being in the spotlight not only means Taylor's romantic relationships and friendships have become well known, but her disagreements and feuds are often brutally public, too.

Her most famous celebrity fall out is probably with rapper Kanye West, with arguments between the two of them dating back over a decade. It began at the 2009 MTV VMA Awards when Taylor, then aged 19, accepted the Best Female Video award for her song 'You Belong With Me', only to find Kanye storm the stage mid-speech and infamously declare "I'mma let you finish" and insist that Beyoncé should have won instead.

"Yo Taylor, I'm really happy for you, I'mma let you finish, but Beyoncé had one of the best videos of all time!" Kanye argued, while Taylor looked on in confusion. Beyoncé herself looked confused too, while the crowd booed and Taylor reportedly left the stage in tears, having had her moment rudely ruined in front of millions of people.

Although Kanye later apologised, the moment stuck in pop culture history and even President Obama labelled him a 'jackass' over the show-stealing move. Kanye later retracted his apology in 2010, and then again in a 2013 interview with *The New York Times*, saying: "I don't have any regret […] If anyone's reading this waiting for some type of full-on, flat apology for anything, they should just stop reading right now."

Things looked to be taking a turn a few years later though when Kanye and Taylor were pictured at the 2015 Grammys together and Kanye even spoke of a collaboration with Taylor. Although what he ended up doing next probably wasn't exactly the kind of collaboration Taylor had in mind…

In February 2016, Kanye released his song 'Famous', which soon became famous for all the wrong reasons after including the line: "I feel like me and Taylor might still have sex. Why? I made that b**** famous." The music video took things a step further, featuring a model of Taylor naked in a giant bed alongside other famous pop culture figures and politicians, including President Trump, Rihanna and *US Vogue* Editor Anna Wintour.

After the line drew criticism, Kanye took to Twitter to defend himself saying that the line was

LEFT: Taylor and her 'squad' of famous friends were the talk of the town in the mid-2010s.

BELOW: The moment of Kanye's infamous interruption of Taylor's speech at the 2009 MTV VMAs.

© John Shearer/Getty Images

actually complimentary. "I called Taylor and had an hour long convo with her about the line, and she thought it was funny and gave her blessings," he tweeted, also claiming that the 'b****' lyric was actually Taylor's idea. Taylor responded to this claim via a spokesperson, saying that she didn't know about the lyric in question but had "cautioned him about releasing a song with such a strong misogynistic message."

Just a few weeks later, when accepting the Album of the Year Grammy for *1989*, Taylor appeared to take a dig at Kanye claiming he had anything to do with her success. "There are going to be people along the way who try to undercut your success or take credit for your accomplishments or your fame – but if you just focus on the work and you don't let those people sidetrack you, someday when you get where you're going, you'll look around and you will know that it was you, and the people who love you, who put you there – and that will be the greatest feeling in the world," she said in her speech.

But things didn't end there. Kanye's wife, Kim Kardashian, released footage allegedly showing Kanye speaking to Taylor on a phone call approving the song, posting it to social media captioned with the snake emoji. Taylor responded by saying that, although she had spoken to Kanye, she had never heard or approved 'Famous', claiming Kanye "promised to play the song for me, but he never did."

"I would very much like to be excluded from this narrative, one that I have never asked to be a part of, since 2009," she ended the statement.

All of this fallout from the past few years – her unfairly scrutinised romantic relationships, the arguments and feuds with some of the people she thought were her friends, and her anger towards a public she often felt abandoned by – were addressed in Taylor's 2017 album *reputation*. Clearing her Instagram ahead of the album's release, she teased the album announcement with videos of snakes and used the imagery throughout the album campaign, even using a giant snake as part of her stage set-up for the album's tour. She wanted to take back the narrative of her being 'a snake' into her own hands.

"A few years ago, someone started an online hate campaign by calling me a snake on the internet.

LEFT: Kanye and Taylor seemed to put their feud behind them at the 2015 MTV VMAs, but it was reignited a few months later when Kanye's 'Famous' was released.

INSET: Taylor used the 'snake' reference during her Reputation Stadium Tour, performing in front of a giant inflatable serpent, nicknamed Karyn.

> "KATY SENT TAYLOR A LITERAL OLIVE BRANCH ON THE OPENING NIGHT OF HER REPUTATION STADIUM TOUR, SEEMINGLY AS AN APOLOGY."

LEFT: Taylor Swift with Katy Perry in 2010, several years before their famous fall out.

RIGHT: Katy Perry making a cameo appearance in Taylor's 'You Need to Calm Down' music video in 2019.

The fact that so many people jumped on board with it led me to feeling lower than I've ever felt in my life, but I can't tell you how hard I had to keep from laughing every time my 63-foot inflatable cobra named Karyn appeared on stage in front of 60,000 screaming fans. It's the stadium tour equivalent of responding to a troll's hateful Instagram comment with 'lol'," she explained in ELLE magazine in 2019.

Taylor's single 'Look What You Made Me Do' appeared to reference her feud with Kanye: "The world moves on, another day another drama, drama. But not for me, not for me, all I think about is karma." The music video also featured Taylor wearing her 2009 VMA outfit, poking fun at herself and repeating the line saying that she "would like to be excluded from this narrative."

The dispute made headlines again in March 2020 when a recording of the phone call between Kanye and Taylor was leaked online. The recording implied that the clip Kim had previously posted was edited, and that Kanye had omitted the term 'b****' when he got Taylor's approval for the line. For Swifties, this was seen as long-overdue vindication for Taylor.

Kanye West isn't the only celebrity that Taylor has had a famous falling out with. She also had a long running feud with Katy Perry, which began in 2014 when Katy allegedly hired some dancers for her 'Prism' tour directly from Taylor's tour. The rumours that the two were feuding only grew when Taylor started talking about the inspiration for her song 'Bad Blood'. Speaking to Rolling Stone, she explained that the track was about "another female artist" that she didn't want to name.

"For years, I was never sure if we were friends or not. She would come up to me at awards shows and say something and walk away, and I would think, 'Are we friends, or did she just give me the harshest insult of my life?'"

Then, the unnamed female pop star crossed a line, Taylor insisted. "She did something so horrible. I was like, 'Oh, we're just straight-up enemies.' And it wasn't even about a guy! It had to do with business. She basically tried to sabotage an entire arena tour. She tried to hire a bunch of people out from under me. And I'm surprisingly non-confrontational – you would not believe how much I hate conflict. So now I have to avoid her. It's awkward, and I don't like it."

In 2017, Katy released 'Swish Swish', a song that some fans think is about Taylor with its lyrics about winning over someone in a fight: "So keep calm, honey, I'mma stick around, for more than a minute, get used to it. Funny my name keeps comin' out your mouth, 'cause I stay winning."

The following year, though, both singers seemed to have made up when Katy sent Taylor a literal olive branch on the opening night of her reputation Stadium Tour, seemingly as an apology. And if that wasn't a clear enough sign that their disagreements were all water under the bridge, in 2019 Katy made an appearance in Taylor's music video for 'You Need to Calm Down'. In this case, it seems like time really can heal all wounds.

DISPUTE WITH SCOOTER BRAUN

In 2019, Taylor had to contend with perhaps her biggest business dispute to be played out publicly so far when Scooter Braun – the music industry heavyweight behind the careers of artists such as Justin Bieber, Ariana Grande, Usher and Kanye West – acquired the masters of her records by buying her former label, Big Machine Label Group, in a deal reported to be worth $300 million.

When Taylor's deal with her first label, Big Machine, came to an end after 12 years in 2018, she had to face the decision of whether to renew the deal or move on to another label. Later that year, she announced she'd signed a multi-album deal with Universal Music Group. Crucially, her new deal with UMG offered her the chance to own her own master recordings of any albums she made for the label.

A 'master' is basically the final version of a song or album, from which all copies of it – vinyls, CDs, digital downloads, streaming files and so on – are made. In Taylor's original deal with Big Machine, she didn't own the masters for the albums she made for the label, but rather earned a percentage of money from any sales or uses of the song while her record label retained ownership of the original master. This is a fairly common part of many artists' deals with a label, as labels want to make sure they can earn back the financial investment they've made in the artist and their music.

Taylor's new deal with UMG offered something slightly different – the right for the label to produce

ABOVE: Big Machine Records' founder and CEO, Scott Borchetta, signed Taylor when she was just 15 years old.

copies of her music to sell, while Taylor still retained the master rights to her work.

This crucial difference is great news for Taylor, as it means she'll have more control over her own music. But the masters of her first six albums still belonged to her old label, something which Taylor wasn't happy with when Scooter Braun bought the label and, with it, her masters.

"When I left my masters in Scott's [CEO of Big Machine] hands, I made peace with the fact that eventually he would sell them. Never in my worst nightmares did I imagine the buyer would be Scooter," she wrote on Tumblr when news of the sale broke on 30 June 2019. "Any time Scott Borchetta has heard the words 'Scooter Braun' escape my lips, it was when I was either crying or trying not to. He knew what he was doing; they both did. Controlling a woman who didn't want to be associated with them. In perpetuity. That means forever."

Taylor had been trying to buy her master recordings for years from Big Machine, she also added, but Scott Borchetta – "someone for whom the term 'loyalty' is clearly a contractual concept"' Taylor insisted – had refused to budge. After her feud with Kanye, who used to be managed by Scooter, this was her worst nightmare.

"All I could think about was the incessant, manipulative bullying I've received at his hands for years," Taylor wrote. "Like when Kim Kardashian orchestrated an illegally recorded snippet of a phone call to be leaked and then Scooter got his two clients together to bully me online about it... Or when his client, Kanye West, organized a revenge porn music video which strips my body naked," she explained. "Now Scooter has stripped me of my life's work, that I wasn't given an opportunity to buy. Essentially, my musical legacy is about to lie in the hands of someone who tried to dismantle it."

Scott denied that he had ever stopped Taylor trying to own her masters, writing in a statement on the Big Machine website: "100% of all Taylor Swift assets were to be transferred to her immediately upon signing the new agreement... My offer to Taylor, for the size of our company, was extraordinary. Taylor and I remained on very good terms when she told me she wanted to speak with other record companies and see what was out there for her. I never got in her way and wished her well."

Scooter, meanwhile, insisted: "I would like to find a resolution... I'm open to ALL possibilities. My attempts and calls to have an open discussion with you over the last six months have all been rejected. While some on your team and many of our mutual friends have tried to get you to the table, all have had no luck. It almost feels as if you have no interest in ever resolving the conflict."

Taylor responded by saying she'd re-record new versions of her old songs, if necessary, and many celebrities rallied around her in support. Selena Gomez wrote on Instagram: "I can tell you first hand the MOST important thing to Taylor is her family, love, her fans, and her MUSIC. I really hope there is a change of heart over this unfortunate situation." Fans started using the hashtag #IStandWithTaylor on Twitter, which quickly became a trending topic.

After regaining the rights to re-record her back catalogue in November 2020, Taylor didn't waste any time; within a year she had released both *Fearless (Taylor's Version)* and *Red (Taylor's Version)*, and has continued amid her busy 2023 touring schedule with the release of *Speak Now (Taylor's Version)*. Through this project, not only has she reclaimed ownership of her songs, she has also raised awareness of the issues surrounding artists' rights in the industry.

At the 2019 AMAs, Taylor made a statement by taking to the stage in a shirt emblazoned with the titles of her first six albums.

CHAPTER 4

STYLE & SUBSTANCE

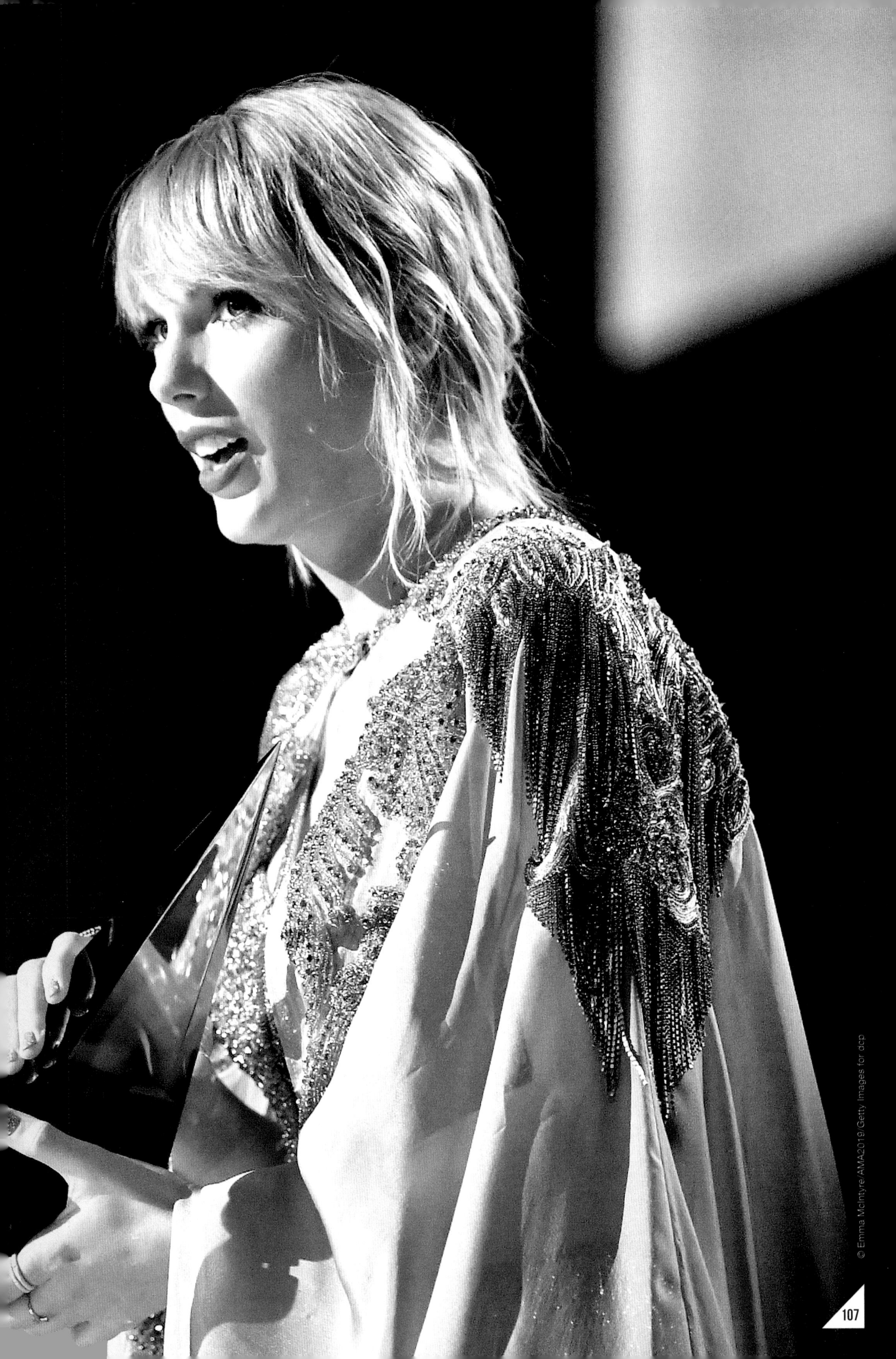

108

STYLE & SUBSTANCE

IN HER JOURNEY TO BECOMING A GLOBAL SUPERSTAR, TAYLOR HAS UNDERGONE A TRANSFORMATION IN SO MANY WAYS, FROM HER EVOLVING FASHION AND AESTHETICS TO HER GROWING INVOLVEMENT IN ACTIVISM AND SOCIAL ISSUES

WORDS BY RACHEL FINN

FASHION EVOLUTION

Growing up in the spotlight meant that Taylor's fashion evolution – from teenager, to twenty-something, and now, as a superstar in her early 30s – was played out for all to see. And as anyone who's ever looked back on their questionable teen fashion choices will be able to tell you, it would be easy to regret some outfits from your younger years – especially when photographic evidence of them exists online!

Taylor, however, seems to take a more laid-back approach. Speaking to *ELLE* magazine in 2015, she talked about how she feels no need to reject any of her former style decisions. "As far as the need to rebel against the idea of you, or the image of you: Like, I feel no need to burn down the house I built by hand," she explained. "I can make additions to it. I can redecorate. But I built this. And so I'm not going to sit there and say, 'Oh, I wish I hadn't had corkscrew-curly hair and worn cowboy boots and sundresses to awards shows when I was 17; I wish I hadn't gone through that fairy-tale phase where I just wanted to wear princess dresses to awards shows every single time.' Because I made those choices. I did that."

Just as Taylor's music has evolved over the years, so has her fashion. When she first began attending red carpet events around the release of her self-titled debut album in 2006, her style was inspired heavily by a country music aesthetic, wearing her hair in tight curls and regularly donning cowboy boots and long, flowing dresses.

Her *Fearless* era added to this and took it further, with her 2009-2010 stadium tour seeing Taylor wear an array of glamorous princess-inspired gowns as a nod towards her *Romeo & Juliet*-inspired 'Love Story' music video and a marching band costume as inspired by her video for 'You Belong With Me', a look that also continued through her *Speak Now* era.

But by the time Taylor got to the release of 2012's *Red*, a move towards a more pop-oriented sound came with a new style. The album's title, predictably, meant Taylor was seen both on-stage and on red-carpets in bold red looks with a splash of red lipstick, but she also veered into classic, clean-cut styles – high-waisted shorts, blouses, stripy tops and a range of stylish hats. It was perhaps the most relatable and practical era of Taylor's fashion journey so far, moving away from the fairytale-inspired looks of her early career and into something a bit more accessible, yet still fashionable. "Every artist has their set of priorities," she told *The Guardian* in 2014. "Being looked at as sexy? Not really on my radar. But nice? I really hope that that is the impression."

If *Red* saw Taylor's style encapsulating a brand of stylish, casual sleek, then *1989* took things in a more glamorous direction again. On her world tour for the album, she wore a showgirl inspired wardrobe, complete with sequined playsuits, crop tops, A-Line skirts and some killer heels. A few years later for her *reputation* tour, she played on the album's dark aesthetic, with black sequinned and snake-print bodysuits and knee-high boots.

One of Taylor's most talked about fashion moments to date was her 2016 Met Gala look. Taylor wore a futuristic silver-panel dress matched with choppy, platinum blonde hair and a deep purple lipstick. On the red carpet, she described herself as a "futuristic gladiator robot" and it was perhaps the most rock 'n' roll-inspired look she's sported to date – and one she carried on for a few months afterwards, looking almost unrecognisable when she appeared on the cover of *Vogue* in May 2016 in sky-high platform boots, a bleach-blonde bob and a glittery slip dress. It was miles away from the girly, country look she was first known for a decade earlier, but Taylor admitted a few years later in an essay she wrote for *ELLE* in 2019, that she wasn't a fan of her brief journey into the style. "If you don't look back at pictures of some of your old looks and cringe, you're doing it wrong," she wrote. "See: Bleachella."

For her seventh album, *Lover*, Taylor's look took inspiration from the rainbow; both her on- and off-stage outfits became softer and lighter, relying heavily on colour and pastels. In comparison to the dark, gothic looks of her *reputation* era, it signalled the biggest change so far for Taylor aesthetically between albums, one she announced by posting a number of cryptic clues on her Instagram – posts that all featured butterflies in some way – right in the run up to the album announcement. If *reputation* played on the idea that Taylor was 'a snake', then it looked like *Lover* was set to be where she spread her wings and flew away from all the drama.

When Taylor surprised the world with her eighth album, *folklore*, her new indie-folk sound was complemented by a relaxed 'cottagecore' style. Where *Lover* was rainbows, *folklore* was neutral, muted shades, and Taylor embraced cosy knitwear, simple dresses and low maintenance hair and makeup. She even released a replica of the cardigan that featured in the music video for 'cardigan' as merchandise, and sent them out as gifts to some famous friends. With each one, she included the note: "I hope this cardigan will keep you warm and cozy in these extremely un-cozy times. Sending you a socially distanced hug and all my love, Taylor."

SYMBOLS AND CLUES

Taylor has long been a fan of creating a rich world for her fans full of clues, symbols and 'Easter eggs' that link her musical worlds together. 'ME!' was the first music video released for *Lover* and it came full of hints to what fans could expect from the rest of the album. The star-studded video featured Big Ben hidden in the horizon of one of the shots (a nod towards album track 'London Boy'), Ellen DeGeneres getting a tattoo that spelled out 'Cruel Summer' on her forearm (based on the album track of the same name) and singer Hayley Kiyoko shooting an arrow into a bullseye that read '5' (a reference to track five: 'The Archer'), among others.

Later, when she released the video for 'The Man' – which marked Taylor's directorial debut and saw her become unrecognisable, transformed by prosthetics to play the role of sleazy businessman 'Tyler Swift' – she filled it with Easter eggs from her personal life. It featured a scene shot in 13th Street Station, a nod to Taylor's favourite number. In reference to her ongoing dispute with music manager Scooter Braun over his acquisition of her former record label Big Machine Label Group (and, with it, the acquisition of the masters of her first six albums), there's a 'no scooters allowed' sign in the subway station and, next to it, one that reads 'MISSING – please return to Taylor Swift', alluding to the fact that she's still fighting to get the rights to her own music.

Previous videos of Taylor's have been full of nods towards her earlier life and career experiences too. In the 2017 video for 'Look What You Made Me Do', Taylor is seen bathing in a bathtub full of jewellery and next to her is a one-dollar bill – a reference to the symbolic $1 Taylor counter-sued former radio DJ David Mueller for over sexual assault in 2016.

FAR LEFT: Taylor's early style was heavily influenced by her country music roots, often performing in cowboy boots.

LEFT: Red carpet events and award shows were an opportunity for the young Taylor to embrace princess-style ballgowns, in keeping with the aesthetic of 'Love Story'.

ABOVE: Taylor has always made time for her fans. Back in June 2010 she held an incredible 13-hour meet and greet event.

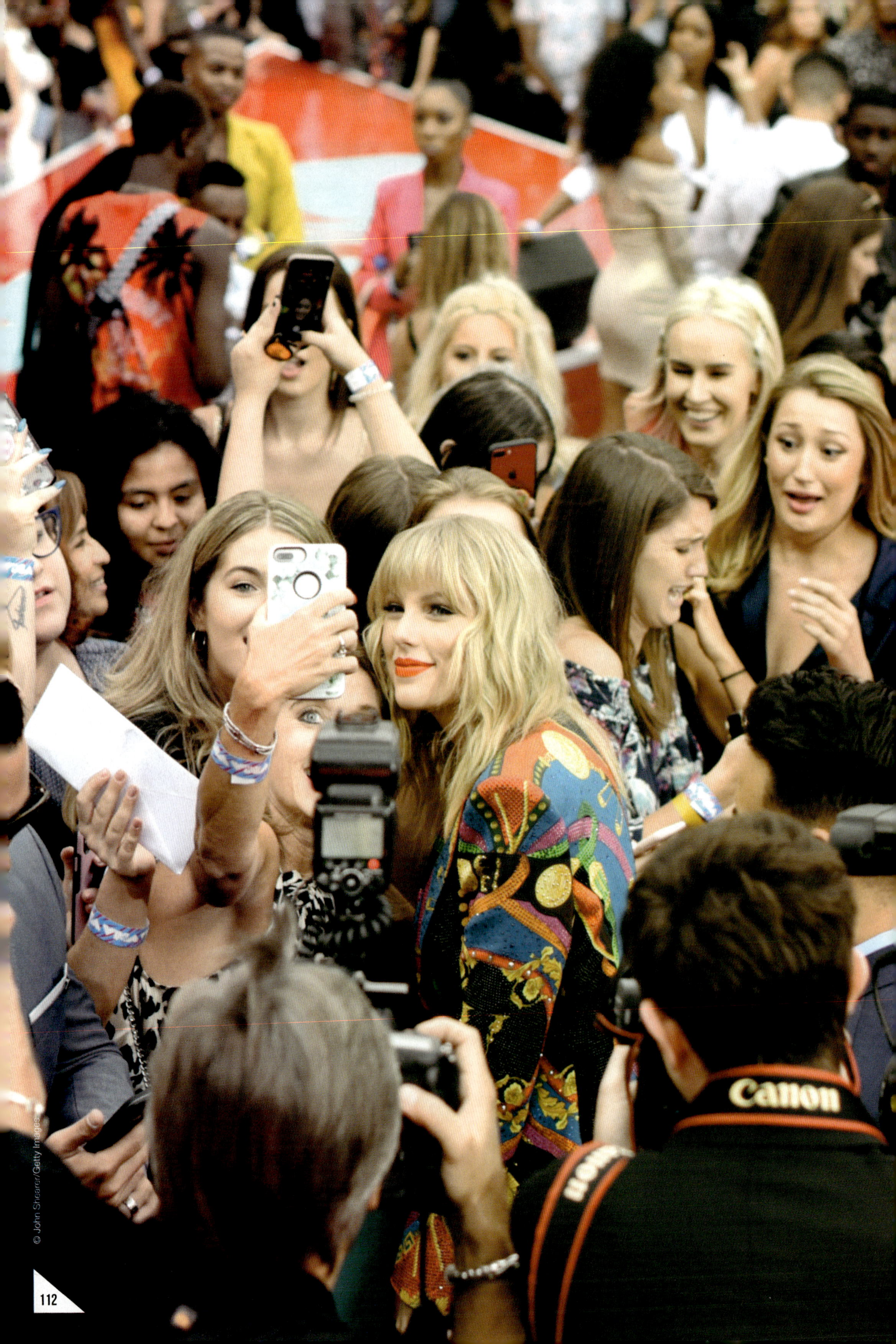
Canon

> **FANS ARE MY FAVOURITE THING IN THE WORLD. I'VE NEVER BEEN THE TYPE OF ARTIST WHO HAS THAT LINE DRAWN BETWEEN THEIR FRIENDS AND THEIR FANS.**
>
> TAYLOR SWIFT

LEFT: Posing for photos with fans on the red carpet for the 2019 MTV VMAs in Newark, New Jersey.

It also features her addressing an army of models – poking fun at those who criticised her 'squad' for being all tall, thin and look-alike. When she crashes a car and is surrounded by paparazzi, she has a hair-style suspiciously similar to Katy Perry's and holds up a Grammy – supposedly joking that Katy has yet to win one (Taylor, meanwhile, has won ten). "I love to communicate through Easter eggs. I think the best messages are cryptic ones," she told *Entertainment Weekly* in 2019.

RELATIONSHIP WITH FANS

All these interlinking messages are fun, of course, but they're also part of Taylor's dedication to her fans and wanting to create a visual and conceptual world that goes beyond just the music. In her early career, much of Taylor's success came from her connection to her fans and the fact that she proved that, rather than just being a genre for adults, country music had an untapped market – teenage girls. Despite not knowing her personally, Taylor's direct and honest lyrics, speaking of heartbreak and unrequited love, mirrored what so many fans would have been going through in their own lives. Rather than dismissing teenage emotions as trivial or over-dramatic, she gave them a voice – often because, as

TOP: During Taylor's *Red* era, she would often be seen wearing something scarlet.

ABOVE: 2014 saw Taylor wave goodbye to her longer locks in favour of a chic bob.

RIGHT: At the 2012 MTV AMAs, Taylor wore a sequinned ringleader costume during her performance of 'We Are Never Ever Getting Back Together'.

a teenager, she was going through the same things that they were too.

"Fans are my favourite thing in the world," she said of her relationship to her fans. "I've never been the type of artist who has that line drawn between their friends and their fans. The line's always been really blurred for me. I'll hang out with them after the show. I'll hang out with them before the show. If I see them in the mall, I'll stand there and talk to them for 10 minutes."

Aside from hanging out with fans IRL after shows, their relationship also extends online. Taylor also joined Tumblr in 2014, sending Swifties thoughtful messages when they were heartbroken, reblogging their funny memes and liking their posts to confirm or deny their theories about albums. She's also sent fans gifts and money to help them pay off student loans or help them out of financial difficulty.

An example of Taylor's impromptu charity made headlines in August 2020, when she donated £23,000 (around $30,000) to Vitoria Mario, a young student in London. Vitoria had moved to the UK from Portugal and was struggling to raise the money she needed to study mathematics at university, since she was not eligible for student loans or grants. She had raised about half of her target amount, when Taylor found her page and wrote the message: "Vitoria, I came across your story online and am so inspired by your drive and dedication to turning your dreams into reality. I want to gift you the rest of your goal amount. Good luck with everything you do! Love, Taylor." Vitoria herself was "over the moon" upon seeing the donation: "She actually made my dream come true."

In a 2012 YouTube video, she explained why she thinks it's so important to give back: "It's honestly one of the most amazing feelings knowing that there's this group of people that has my back, and that they always show up. I try to figure out ways all the time to thank them for that."

Taylor's music has no doubt helped so many of her fans through some of life's most difficult moments, but in turn they've also never hesitated to rally around her in moments of crisis. In a plea posted to Twitter after Scooter Braun acquired her old masters in 2019, she wrote: "This is where I'm asking for your help. Please let [Big Machine founder] Scott Borchetta and Scooter Braun know how you feel about this." Fans mobilised with the hashtag #IStandWithTaylor and sent thousands of messages to Scott and Scooter, asking them to be fair to her in their disagreement.

Not all of Taylor's fans are, well, human though. It's no secret to anyone – fan or not – that Taylor is a cat lady (and we mean that as a compliment!) She has three cats: Meredith Grey, Olivia Benson and Benjamin Button. The first to be added to Taylor's feline family in 2011 was Meredith, an adopted kitten, named after a character in the TV series *Grey's Anatomy*, one of her favourite shows. In 2014, she got Olivia, named after the character in *Law & Order* and, in 2019, Benjamin Button, named after the character portrayed by Brad Pitt in the 2008 film *The Curious Case of Benjamin Button*. "They can say whatever they want about my personal life because I know what my personal life is, and it involves a lot of TV and cats and girlfriends," she joked in an interview with *The Guardian* in 2014.

ACTIVISM

Although Taylor first shot to fame writing about her personal life and keeping her career mostly about her music, as she got older, she began to turn her view outwards, speaking out on many political issues that she'd previously been reluctant to talk about – although this wasn't after until she'd gone through a period where she felt under more and more pressure to speak out.

Unlike many celebrities, Taylor didn't explicitly endorse a candidate for the 2016 US presidential election, leading many to believe that, at best, she didn't really care or, at worst, she was actually a secret supporter of right-wing Republican candidate Donald Trump. As the run-up to the election was underway, Taylor seemed busy doing other things, posting pictures of herself on Instagram attending New York Fashion Week, posing with Drake, cuddling koalas and even partying with her celebrity friends waving an American flag at one of her 4th of July parties – all while keeping quiet about any political opinions one way or another. Some fans feared that she was keeping quiet due to fears of alienating parts of her fan-base, something which may have happened considering her background in country music, a genre which has historically been popular with many Southern conservative voters. She didn't mention the election publicly at all until the day itself, when she posted a photo of herself queuing to vote with the caption: "Today is the day. Go out and VOTE."

Then it all changed. A few years later, Taylor spoke of her regret of not being more openly political and how, going forward, she wanted to speak out for things she thought were right. In conversation with *The Guardian* in 2019, she explained: "The things that happen to you in your life are what develop your political opinions. I was living in this Obama eight-year paradise of, you go, you cast your vote, the person you vote for wins, everyone's happy! This whole thing, the last three, four years, it completely blindsided a lot of us, me included."

When her next chance to vote came around, this time she didn't keep quiet. After she posted to Instagram to endorse the Democratic candidate Phil Bredesen from her hometown of Tennessee for the 2018 senate race, she caused a surge in people registering to vote, with more than 65,000 new registrations in the 24 hours following her post (an effect the media called the 'Swift Lift'). Donald Trump's response? "Let's say that I like Taylor's music about 25% less now."

"I hate to admit this, but I felt that I wasn't educated enough on it," she later explained. "Because I hadn't actively tried to learn about politics in a way that I felt was necessary for me, making statements that go out to hundreds of millions of people."

But now Taylor is older and wiser, and things have changed. In the run up to the 2020 presidential election, she has made her political allegiances crystal clear and continues to encourage people to make sure they vote. Responding to Trump's attempts to undermine the postal voting system (with record numbers expected to vote by mail during the ongoing Covid-19 pandemic), she took to Twitter: "Trump's calculated dismantling of USPS proves one thing clearly: He is WELL AWARE that we do not want him as our president. He's chosen to blatantly cheat and put millions of Americans' lives at risk in an effort to hold on to power." Following up with: "Donald Trump's ineffective leadership

FAR LEFT: As Taylor transitioned from teenager to twenty-something, she started to include more classic styles in her wardrobe.

LEFT: Taylor's striking outfit for the 2016 Met Gala, which had the theme 'Manus x Machina: Fashion In An Age Of Technology'. She would later jokingly refer to this look as 'Bleachella'.

RIGHT: Taylor's *reputation* wardrobe reflected the darker themes of the album.

"I WAS LIVING IN THIS OBAMA EIGHT-YEAR PARADISE OF, YOU GO, YOU CAST YOUR VOTE, THE PERSON YOU VOTE FOR WINS..."

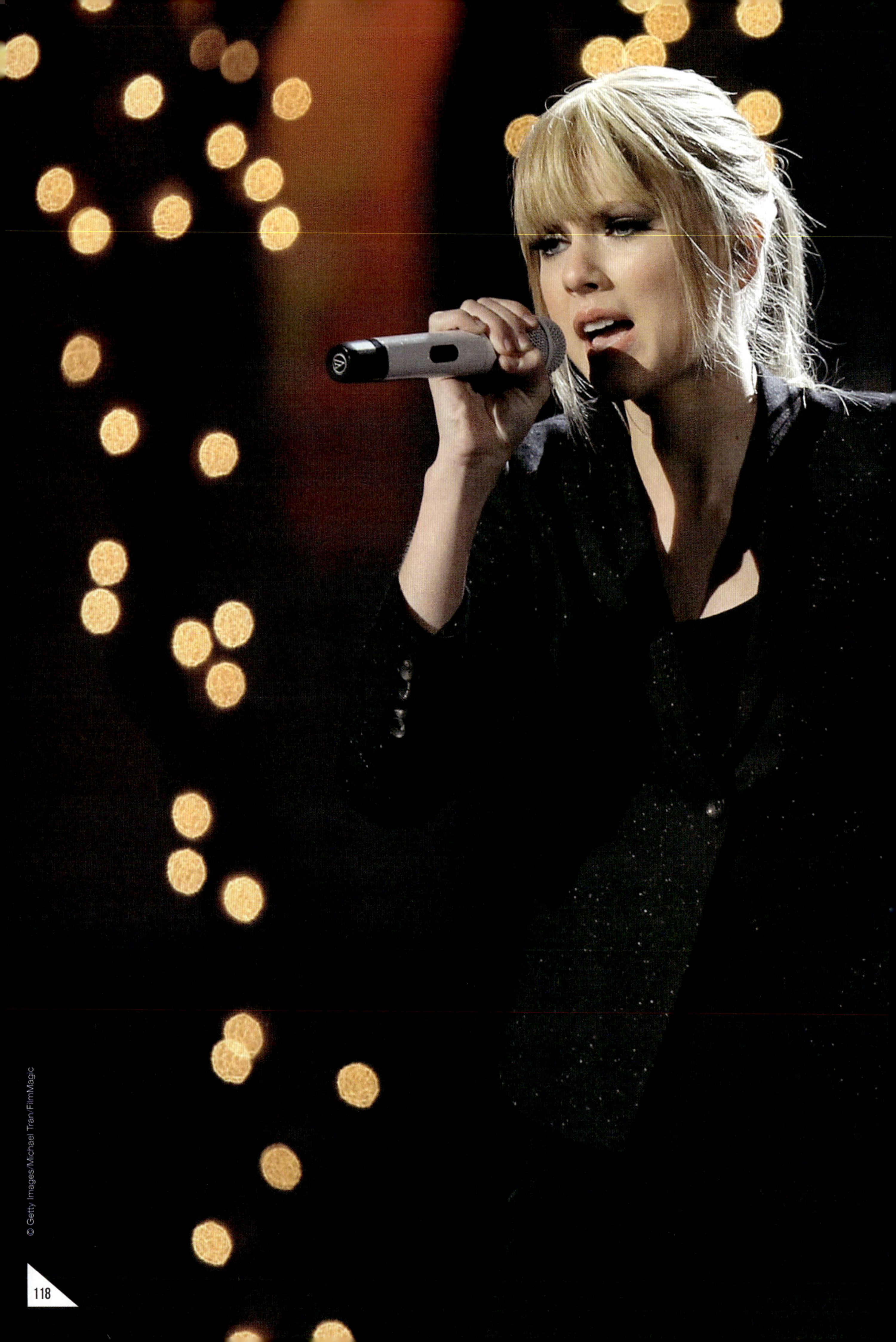

With a sleek black suit and poker-straight hair, Taylor's look for the 2010 American Music Awards was quite the change from her trademark dresses and curls.

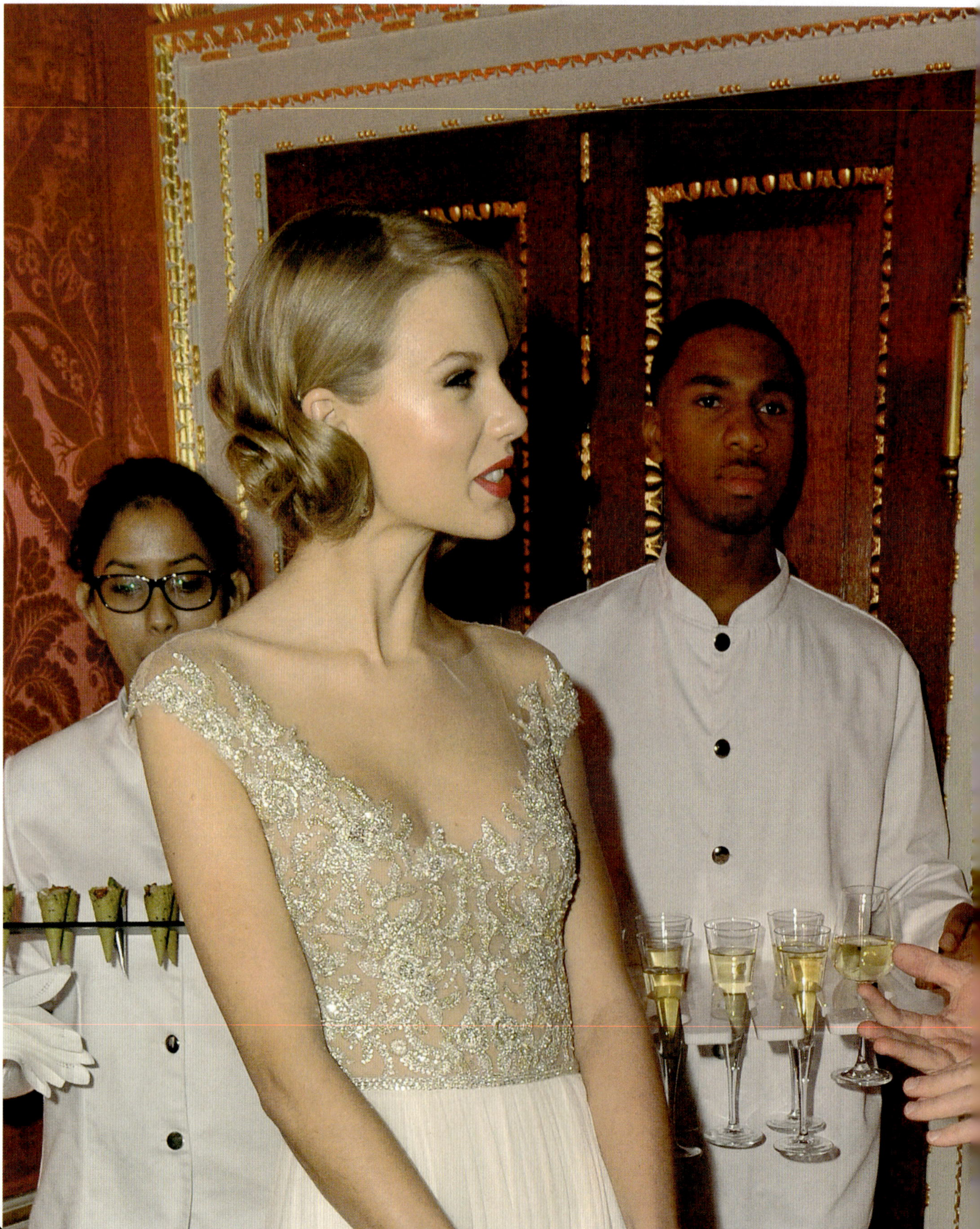

gravely worsened the crisis that we are in and he is now taking advantage of it to subvert and destroy our right to vote and vote safely. Request a ballot early. Vote early." It's clear to see that Taylor is no longer holding back!

Voting isn't the only area Taylor has been speaking out about more in recent years. She first made a call for gun control in March 2018, donating an undisclosed amount of money for the March For Our Lives Rally, a student-led movement against gun violence that was founded by survivors of the Stoneman Douglas High School shooting. "No one should have to go to school in fear of gun violence. Or to a nightclub. Or to a concert. Or to a movie theater. Or to their place of worship," Taylor wrote in an Instagram caption. The rally's turnout was estimated to be between 1.2-2 million people, making it one of the largest protests in American history. "I've made a donation to show my support for the students, for the March For Our Lives campaign, for everyone affected by these tragedies, and to support gun reform," she added.

In 2017, after she went to court to defend herself against radio DJ David Mueller – who was fired from his job after allegedly groping Taylor during a meet-and-greet in 2013 – she also found herself in the midst of another important social and political movement. Not long after, in October 2017 the hashtag #MeToo went viral, with women (and some men) around the world sharing their experiences of sexual harassment and assault, following the widespread abuse allegations against now-disgraced film producer Harvey Weinstein. Taylor's story became one of many discussed in the movement, with *TIME* magazine including her in their Person Of The Year 2017 special as one of their 'Silence Breakers', which documented a range of people across different industries and backgrounds who'd stood up against harassment and assault. "I think that this moment is important for awareness, for how parents are talking to their children, and how victims are processing their trauma, whether it be new or old," Taylor explained in an Instagram post. "The brave women and men who have come forward this year have all moved the needle in terms of letting people know that this abuse of power shouldn't be tolerated."

Taylor is also outspoken on LGBTQ+ discrimination, something she addresses directly in her single 'You

LEFT: Prince William talks with Taylor during the Winter Whites Gala dinner in aid of the youth homelessness charity Centrepoint at Kensington Palace in London, 2013.

RIGHT: Taylor pictured in 2014 with one of her three pet cats, Scottish fold Olivia Benson.

BELOW: Swift fans displayed messages of support in the windows of a building across the street during Taylor's court case against David Mueller.

FAR RIGHT: Kerry Kennedy, Vincent A Mai and Frank Mugisha attend the Robert F Kennedy Center with Taylor for the 2012 Justice and Human Rights Ripple of Hope gala in New York.

FAR RIGHT, BELOW: Shortly after breaking her political silence in an Instagram post, Taylor used her acceptance speech at the 2018 AMAs to encourage people to vote in the US midterm elections.

Need To Calm Down' from *Lover*, with the lyrics: "You just need to take several seats and then try to restore the peace, and control your urges to scream about all the people you hate, 'cause shade never made anybody less gay." She also created a petition in support of the pro-LGBT 'Equality Act' that she shared at the end of the song's star-studded video (to date, it has over 800,000 signatures) and, thanks to the lyric "Why are you mad? When you could be GLAAD?", the release of the song also led to a rise in donations to GLAAD, an anti-LGBT discrimination charity. Many fans gave symbolic donations of $13, in reference to Taylor's lucky number.

Although Taylor has been more outspoken about LGBTQ+ rights in more recent years, she's spoken about regretting that she hadn't done more in the past. "Maybe a year or two ago, [my friend] Todrick [Hall] and I are in the car, and he asked me, "What would you do if your son was gay?"" she told *Vogue* in 2019. "The fact that he had to ask me… shocked me and made me realize that I had not made my position clear enough or loud enough. If my son was gay, he'd be gay. I don't understand the question."

"If he was thinking that, I can't imagine what my fans in the LGBTQ+ community might be thinking," she added. "It was kind of devastating to realise that I hadn't been publicly clear about that."

In June 2020, when global protests broke out after the death of George Floyd, a black man from Minneapolis who was wrongfully killed by a police officer after allegedly trying to use a counterfeit note, Taylor also didn't stay silent, using her platform to speak out about lack of police accountability over racist behaviour. "Racial injustice has been ingrained deeply into local and state governments, and changes must be made there. In order for policies to change, we need to elect people who will fight against police brutality and racism of any kind," she tweeted alongside the Black Lives Matter hashtag. In a tweet to Donald Trump, she added: "After stoking the fires of white supremacy and racism your entire presidency, you have the nerve to feign moral superiority before threatening violence? We will vote you out in November." The message has since been liked over 2 million times.

Taylor's journey from a teenager that first won over fans with her honest and personal account of teenage life to a global superstar advocating for some of the world's most important issues is sure a sign of her growing influence around the world, but also reminds us of something else: the importance of speaking out for what's right, even when it doesn't affect us directly. As Taylor summed up to *Vogue* in 2019: "I didn't realise until recently that I could advocate for a community that I'm not a part of."

> **"I ENJOYED BEING ABLE TO HELP HER REALISE THAT USING HER VOICE IS A HUMONGOUS INSTRUMENT THAT IS ABLE TO CHANGE THE MINDS OF THOSE WHO, WITHOUT HER, MAY HAVE NEVER LOOKED AT GAY PEOPLE AS ACTUAL PEOPLE."**
>
> TODRICK HALL ON HIS FRIENDSHIP WITH TAYLOR

RIGHT: Taylor and Todrick Hall backstage at the Broadway production of *Kinky Boots* in 2016.

125

CHAPTER 5

SUPERSTAR

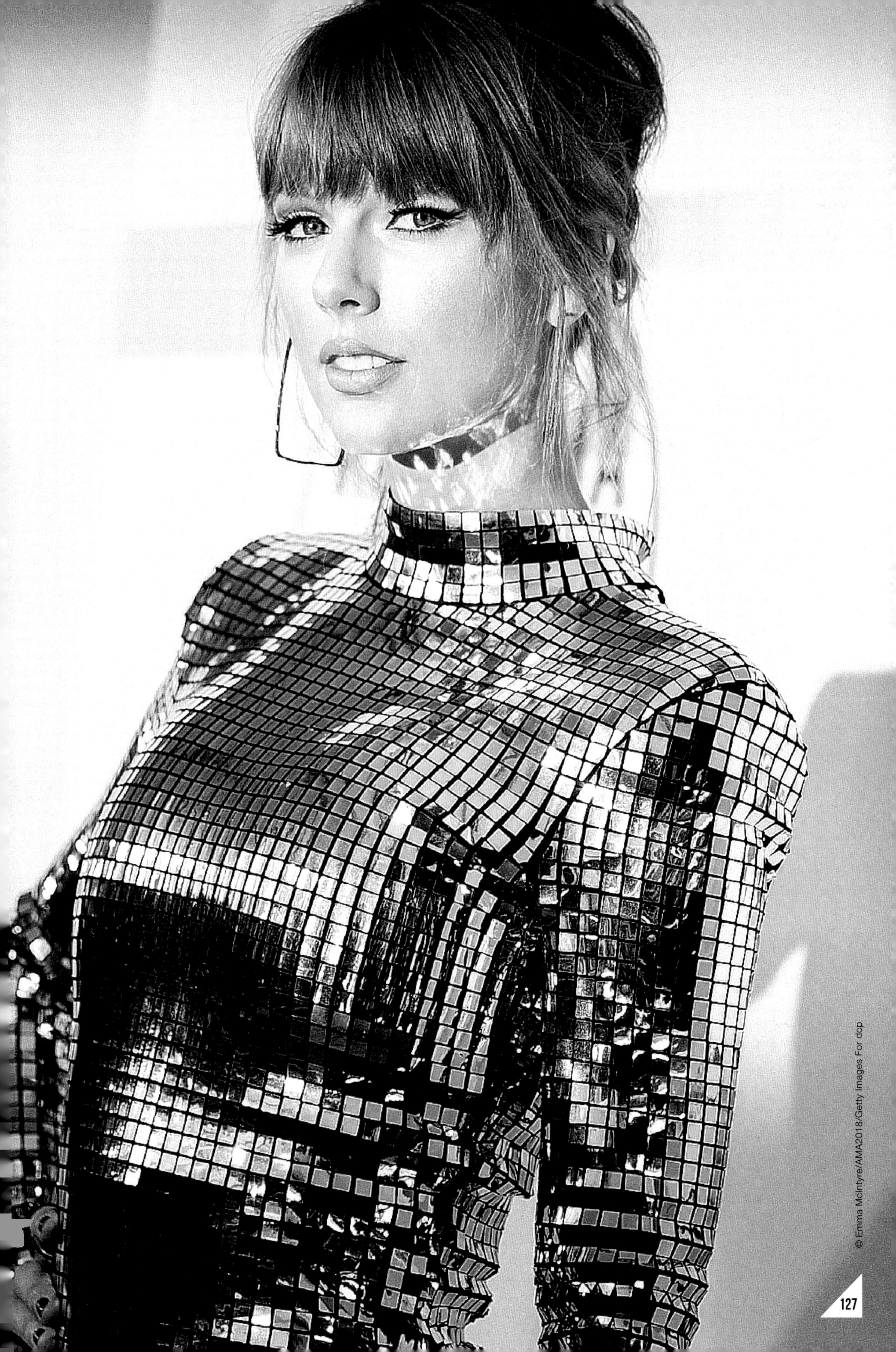

SUPERSTAR

ALL TAYLOR'S SUCCESSES HAVE MADE HER ONE OF THE MOST INFLUENTIAL POP CULTURE ICONS IN THE WORLD – AND SHE SHOWS NO SIGN OF SLOWING DOWN

WORDS BY RACHEL FINN

AWARDS AND ACCOLADES

In her career to date, Taylor has racked up a truly astounding number of accolades, having won over 500 awards and been nominated for over 1,100 more. As of April 2023, she's won 12 Grammys so far, and became the first female artist in history to win three Album of the Year Grammys. In fact, she's now tied for the record of Most Album of the Year awards with Frank Sinatra, Stevie Wonder, and Paul Simon. She's also won two BRIT awards, including the prestigious Global Icon award, has won 26 Teen Choice Awards, plus an Emmy for her concert film *AMEX Unstaged: Taylor Swift Experience* in 2015. That's not forgetting 16 People's Choice Awards, three NME awards, 14 MTV VMAs, 40 American Music Awards, eight Academy of Country Music Awards, and many, *many* more.

If that wasn't enough, Taylor's also broken a whole host of Guinness World Records, including 'Biggest-selling album worldwide for a solo artist' for 2019's *Lover*, 'Most million-selling weeks on US albums charts' for three consecutive albums (*Speak Now*, *Red* and *1989*), and 'Highest annual earnings for a musician ever (female)', with estimated earnings of $185 million between June 2018 and June 2019. In 2020, the release of *folklore* broke the record for 'Most day-one streams of an album on Spotify' for a female artist.

In 2019, Taylor's long list of achievements culminated in two major awards, celebrating Taylor's first full decade in music. She was named Artist of the Decade at the American Music Awards as well as Billboard's Woman of the Decade. For the latter, Taylor used her acceptance speech to give a passionate talk about the struggles and successes she's faced in the industry as well as talking about the importance of nurturing and looking after the younger female pop stars who will come after her.

"In the last ten years I have watched as women in this industry are criticised and measured up to each other and picked at for their bodies, their romantic lives, their fashion..." she said. "Have you ever heard someone say that about a male artist? 'I really like his songs but I don't know what it is, there's just something about him I don't like?' No! That criticism is reserved for us!"

"It seems like the pressure that could have crushed us made us into diamonds instead," she continued. "And what didn't kill us actually did make us stronger. But we need to keep advocating for women in the recording studios, behind the mixing board, in A&R meetings, because rather than fighting to be taken seriously in their fields, these women are still struggling to even have a chance to be in the room."

In the speech, she also spoke about the intense pressure she's faced from the public and the media and how difficult it can be to meet the impossible standards placed on women in the public eye. "They're saying I'm dating too much in my 20s? Okay, I'll stop, I'll just be single. For years. Now they're saying my album *Red* is filled with too many breakup songs? Okay, okay, I'll make one about moving to New York and deciding that really my life is more fun with just my friends. Oh, they're saying my music is changing too much for me to stay in country music? All right. Okay, here's an entire genre shift and a pop album called *1989*. Now it's that I'm showing you too many pictures of me with my friends, okay, I can stop doing that too. Now I'm actually a calculated manipulator rather than a smart businesswoman? Okay, I'll disappear from public view for years. Now I'm being cast as a villain

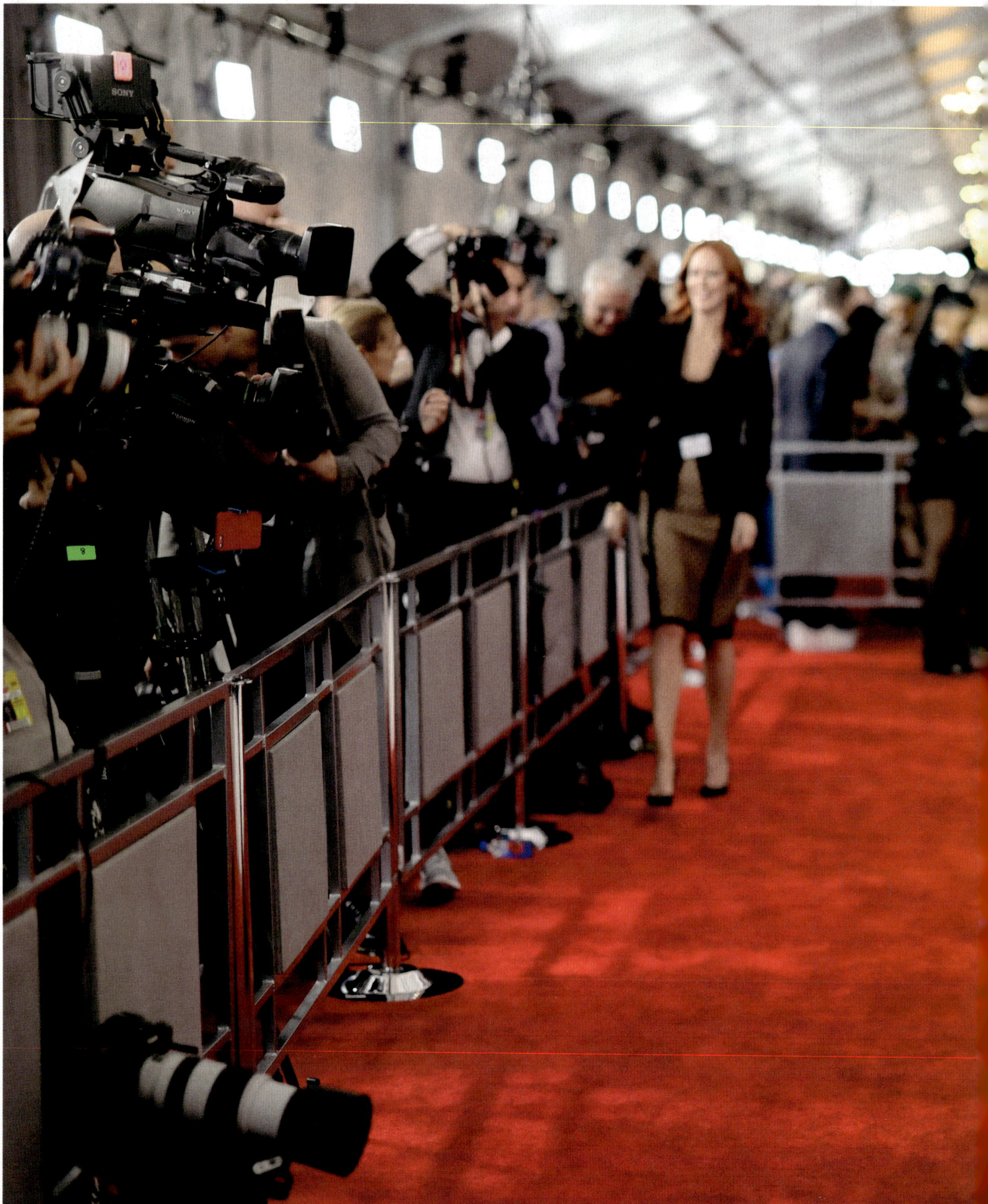
SONY

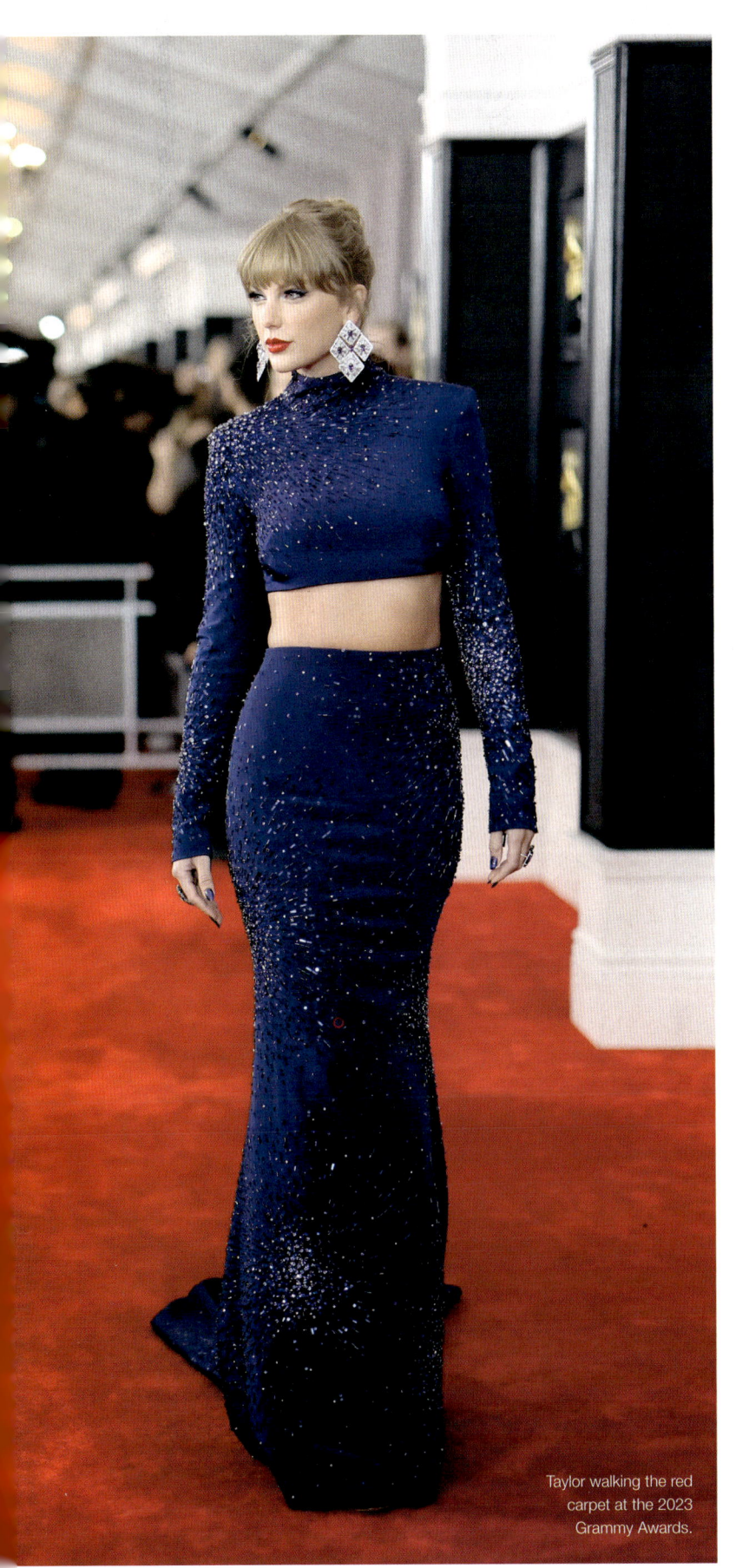

Taylor walking the red carpet at the 2023 Grammy Awards.

to you? Okay, here's an album called *reputation* and there are lots of snakes everywhere."

HITTING THE BIG SCREEN

As well as her music career, Taylor has also ventured into acting, appearing in various TV shows and films throughout her career. Her first role was in a 2009 episode of *CSI*, where she played Hayley Jones, a rebellious teenager who is killed in suspicious circumstances. She dyes her hair various dark shades, has a lip piercing and has a drug dealing boyfriend – quite the opposite of Taylor in real life!

CSI may have been Taylor's small-screen debut but she made her first appearance in a feature film in 2010's *Valentine's Day*, a romantic comedy following a group of interlinking people and their struggles with love on one February 14th. Taylor plays Felicia, the annoying and over-enthusiastic high school girlfriend of William, as they navigate their first ever relationship. William was played by Taylor's ex-boyfriend Taylor Lautner (fans dubbed them 'Taylor squared') and the film was how they first met. They dated for a few months while making the film in 2009 but had split up by the time it came out the following year. Taylor (Lautner, that is) later admitted that the other Taylor's song 'Back To December' was about their relationship. "He's one of my best friends," Taylor explained to *Glamour* in 2011 about their split. "He's wonderful, and we'll always be close. I'm so thankful for that."

In 2012, Taylor starred alongside Zac Efron in animated film *The Lorax*, playing tree-loving daydreamer Audrey in the adaption of the Dr Seuss classic. Unlike her live music performances or previous acting roles, the film saw Taylor face the challenge of voicing an animated character for the first time. "It's a completely different space that you go to in your head," she explained about voice-over work. "It's very different from when you're singing songs that you wrote. With this, you're sitting there in a booth by yourself having conversations with no one."

The following year Taylor had a small role in the season 2 finale of *New Girl* and the year after that made a move into science-fiction with *The Giver*, playing the supporting role of Rosemary – a young woman who experiences all the memories of a society in a post-apocalyptic future where emotion has been suppressed. Viewers may have taken a while to spot her though as she appears on screen with her usual blonde hair a shade of deep brunette!

Perhaps Taylor's most discussed role to date though is her appearance in *Cats*. The on-screen adaptation of the Andrew Lloyd Webber musical included a star-studded cast alongside Taylor, with appearances from James Corden, Judi Dench, Jason Derulo, Idris Elba, Rebel Wilson and more, with Taylor playing the role of Bombalurina. Her big moment comes towards the end of the film when she sings the song 'Macavity' from the musical in a British accent, before sprinkling catnip all over the other cats. And that's about it!

Her screen-time in the actual film may only stretch to a few minutes, but Taylor was more involved behind the scenes of the film, teaming up with its creator Andrew Lloyd Webber to write a new song for the film called 'Beautiful Ghosts'. It's performed in the film by the main character (or should that be main cat?) Victoria, who's played by ballet dancer Francesca Hayward. Judi Dench's character Old Deuteronomy also performs a scaled-back version of the song later in the film and we hear Taylor's full version of the song in the credits. According to Taylor, the song is about trying to find a sense of belonging: "'Beautiful Ghosts' is sung from a young voice who is wondering if she will ever have glory days. Longing for the sense of belonging she sees everyone finding. Reaching for it, desperately afraid of never having beautiful ghosts of days gone by to cling to in her older years."

The film became controversial when released in 2019 after being panned by many critics and estimated to have made its creator Universal pictures a loss of between $71–114 million. Taylor, however, said she just loved the experience of being part of the film. "I had a really great time working on that weird-ass movie," she told *Variety*. "I'm not gonna retroactively decide that it wasn't the best experience. I never would have met Andrew Lloyd Webber or gotten to see how he works, and now he's my buddy. I got to work with the sickest dancers and performers. No complaints."

But although Taylor has undertaken a range of acting roles, it's clear music is still her one true love and she'll only go for roles she really connects with, rather than doing it just for fame or money (arguably she's got enough of both already anyway!) "When I look at acting careers that I really admire, I see that it's been a precise decision-making process for these

RIGHT: Taylor is pictured with her fellow *Cats* star, Idris Elba, at the film's world premiere in New York. The singer co-wrote and recorded the song 'Beautiful Ghosts' for the film.

people," she explained. "They make decisions based on what they love, and they do only the things that they are passionate about. They play only characters that they can't stop thinking about."

POWER IN THE MUSIC BUSINESS

As well as using her influence to speak out about political and social issues over the past few years, Taylor has also leveraged her power to speak out about the struggles of those who work in the music industry – particularly artists – in a bid to pave the way for younger and less experienced artists entering the industry after her.

She famously had a 'boycott' of Spotify between 2014 and 2017, pulling her albums from the streaming service to make a stand against what she said was unfair payment to music creators. Explaining the decision to Yahoo!, Taylor said: "All I can say is that music is changing so quickly, and the landscape of the music industry itself is changing so quickly, that everything new, like Spotify, all feels to me a bit like a grand experiment. And I'm not willing to contribute my life's work to an experiment that I don't feel fairly compensates the writers, producers, artists, and creators of this music. And I just don't agree with perpetuating the perception that music has no value and should be free... I thought, 'I will try this; I'll see how it feels.' It didn't feel right to me."

It's difficult to calculate exactly how much a streaming service might pay an artist per stream of a song as it's often based on a variety of factors, such as the listener's location, whether the subscriber has a free or paid-for account, the royalty rate a specific artist may have negotiated and the relative pricing or currency conversion between different regions. However, streaming services have often come under fire for not paying creators a fair share for the work they produce, especially when contrasted to physical music sales. Spotify, in particular, is estimated to only pay $0.004 (or about £0.003)

133

"TAYLOR HAS RACKED UP A TRULY ASTOUNDING NUMBER OF ACCOLADES, HAVING WON OVER 400 AWARDS AND BEEN NOMINATED FOR ALMOST 1,000 MORE."

Taylor won in six categories at the 2019 American Music Awards, becoming the most awarded artist in the history of the AMAs with 29 wins. As of 2022, she has extended this record with a remarkable 40 wins.

© ANGELA WEISS/AFP via Getty Images

per stream – not exactly a huge amount, when everyone including the artist, songwriter, producer and record label takes their cut! The system makes things particularly challenging for emerging artists, who may struggle to receive the many thousands of streams required to make a reasonable profit.

She didn't stop at limiting her criticism to Spotify either. In June 2015, Taylor criticised Apple Music, when it was discovered that they wouldn't be paying artists any royalties for streams that happened during users' three-month free trial period, calling it 'shocking' and 'disappointing'. Taking to Tumblr, Taylor wrote: "This is not about me. Thankfully I am on my fifth album and can support myself, my band, crew, and entire management team by playing live shows. This is about the new artist or band that has just released their first single and will not be paid for its success. This is about the young songwriter who just got his or her first cut and thought that the royalties from that would get them out of debt."

Just a few days later, Apple Music backed down and announced it would pay royalties to everyone throughout its free trial period. The following week Taylor then announced that she'd be streaming her back catalogue, including new album *1989*, on the platform after all. "This is simply the first time it's felt right in my gut to stream my album," she tweeted. "Thank you, Apple, for your change of heart." When she then appeared in an advert for Apple in 2016 – which showed her running on (and subsequently falling off of) a treadmill while listening to an Apple Music-curated playlist called "#GYMFLOW" – it seemed their disagreement was well and truly over.

Taylor's music was put back on Spotify in June 2017. While she may not have managed to negotiate higher streaming payments for artists, she did manage to do something pretty amazing for them when signing a new record deal with Universal Music in 2018. After her first record deal with Big Machine Group ended that year, Taylor decided to sign a new record deal with Universal Music Group and Republic Records. But, unusually for a record deal, Taylor's contract proposed that the label must promise to hand over to its artists a proportion of any money it makes from any future sales of the shares it owns in Spotify – and the label agreed. Taylor said that the agreement "meant more to me than any other deal point" of her new contract, which also gave her ownership of her masters going

LEFT: At the Z100 iHeartRadio Jingle Ball in December 2019, Taylor was presented with a huge cake – complete with photos of her beloved cats – to celebrate her 30th birthday.

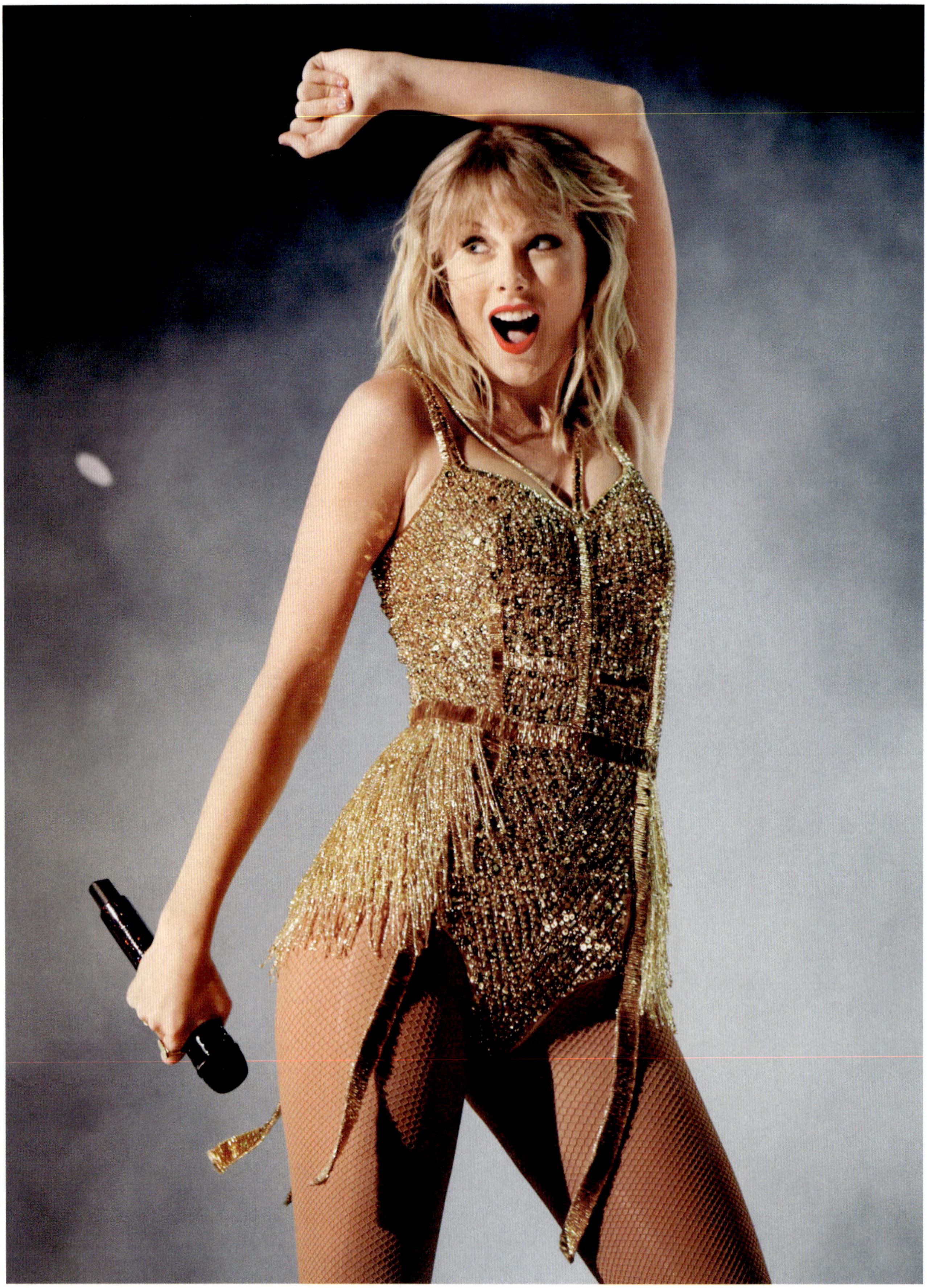

© John Shearer / AMA2019 / Getty Images for dcp

forward. "We are headed toward positive change for creators – a goal I'm never going to stop trying to help achieve, in whatever ways I can."

As well as speaking out on the importance of artists getting fairly compensated for their work, Taylor has also spoken about how she fights to make the music industry a fairer place so that younger women are supported. When accepting Billboard's Woman of the Year award in 2014, she said: "I really just feel like we need to continue to try to offer something to a younger generation of musicians, because somewhere right now your future Woman of the Year is probably sitting in a piano lesson or in a girls' choir and today right now we need to take care of her."

When she walked onto the Billboard stage once again years later to accept their Woman of the Decade award, she referred back to that 2014 speech. "I've since learned that at that exact moment, an 11-year-old girl in California really was taking piano lessons and really was in a girls' choir. And this year she has been named Woman of the Year at the age of 17. Her name is Billie [Eilish]," she reflected. "And those are the stories we need to think about every day as we do our jobs within this industry. The ones where people's dreams come true and they get to create music and play it for people. The ones where fans feel a connection to music that makes their day easier, makes their night more fun, makes their love feel more sacred, or their heartache feel less isolating."

It's not just young female pop stars that Taylor has had an effect on, but young women of all levels interested in playing music. In 2018, guitar

ABOVE: Taylor was given the honour of inducting legendary songwriter Carole King into the Rock & Roll Hall of Fame in 2021.

LEFT: Taylor always wows the crowds, whether singing at the piano or performing high-energy choreography.

manufacturing company Fender found that 50% of new guitar sales were being driven by young women in something they called the 'Taylor Swift factor'. This suggested that, although Taylor's newer music has moved further away from the country-driven guitar sound which first made her famous, it's still having an effect on girls all over the world.

MISS AMERICANA
One of the most intimate insights into Taylor's life and career came in January 2020 in the form of documentary *Miss Americana*. The Lana Wilson-directed film follows Taylor over the course of several years through a range of interviews, flashbacks, home videos and concert footage filmed across the making of her sixth and seventh albums, *reputation* and *Lover*.

Despite Taylor's polished and confident appearance, the film dives deep into her inner thoughts and reveals that she puts an incredible amount of pressure on herself – to make good music, to be good to her fans and, as she describes at one point, to "be thought of as good."

"My entire moral code is a need to be thought of as good," she admits early in the film. "I was so fulfilled by approval, that that was it. I became the person who everyone wanted me to be." In one particularly revealing moment, when finding out *reputation* has not been nominated for any of the Grammys' major categories, instead of defending the album she simply states: "This is fine. I need to make a better record."

The documentary also sees Taylor talk candidly about the fact that, despite all her success, she isn't immune to feeling isolated or lonely. Instead, that success can sometimes create a distance between herself and those around her and leave her with difficulty finding someone to relate to. Talking about winning Album of the Year for the second time at the Grammys, she admits: "That was it – my life had never been better. That was all you wanted. That was all you focused on... [But] you get to the mountain-top and you look around and you're like, 'Oh God, what now?' I didn't have a partner that I'd climbed it with that I could high-five. I didn't have anyone I could talk to who could relate to... I had my mom, but I just wondered, shouldn't I have someone that I could call right now?"

She also admits for the first time her struggle with disordered eating, something that was magnified by being in the public eye. In an honest admission in the back of a car in one scene, she explains: "I've learned over the years that it's not good for me to see pictures of myself every day... I tend to get triggered by something, whether it's a picture of

In recent years, Taylor has also turned her hand to directing. She has directed several of her own music videos, as well as a short film based on her song 'All Too Well'.

me where I feel like my tummy was too big or like someone said I looked pregnant or something, and that will just trigger me to starve a little bit. Just stop eating."

Thankfully, over time, it's something she's learned to cope with. "I'm a lot happier with who I am," she adds. "I don't care as much if, like, somebody points out that I have gained weight. It's just something that makes my life better, the fact that I'm a size 6 instead of a size 00."

The documentary also gives fans more insight into the dark side of fame, revealing that in one particularly grim incident a stalker broke into her apartment... and slept in her bed! The weird revelation comes to light during candid footage of Taylor recording 'ME!' with Panic! at the Disco's Brendon Urie. It was one of many incidents that led to finally be more open in her politics and speak out against Tennessee senator Marsha Blackburn, who voted against reauthorising the Violence Against Women Act, as well as voting against gay marriage.

Her decision to speak out politically was not supported by everyone on her team, who worried that it would turn the public against her. Taylor mentions the example of The Chicks, who experienced a huge backlash when they criticised President Bush over the invasion of Iraq in 2003, having their music blacklisted from country music stations and receiving death threats over their comments in America's then post-9/11 patriotic landscape. "I want to love glitter and also stand up for the double standards that exist in our society," the singer says later in the film. "I want to wear pink and tell you how I feel about politics. I don't think those things have to cancel each other out... I need to be on the right side of history."

The film also has some heartwarming moments though, and sees her speaking about her relationship with then partner Joe Alwyn. Although Joe does appear briefly in the film, seen giving her a hug after a concert, he's not featured too much – something Taylor admits is because of their decision to keep their relationship to themselves. "I also was falling in love with someone who had a really wonderfully normal, balanced, grounded life," she reveals. "And we decided together that we wanted our relationship to be private." In one particularly cute moment, we see Taylor sweetly mouth 'I love you' to Joe as he films her singing *reputation* track 'Call It What You Want' on her guitar at home. After years of sharing so much of herself with everyone and sourcing her happiness from other people's opinions of her, their relationship helped her find happiness without the influence of other people. "I wasn't happy in the way I was trained to be happy.

© Dimitrios Kambouris / Getty Images

141

ABOVE: *folklore* and *evermore*'s stories and dreamscapes offered fans some much-needed escapism during the pandemic.

BELOW: In September 2022, Taylor was named Songwriter-Artist of the Decade at the NSAI Nashville Songwriter Awards.

It was happiness without anyone else's input. It's… just… we were happy."

At home, during a dinner with her childhood best friend, Abigail, where they discuss friends of theirs who have recently had children, she shares her own thoughts on having a family of her own one day. "There's a part of me that feels like I'm 57 years old, but another part of me that's, like, definitely not ready to have kids, not ready for all this grown-up stuff," she says. "I kind of don't really have the luxury of just figuring stuff out because my life is planned, like, two years ahead of time. In two months they'll come to me with the dates for the next tour."

WHAT'S NEXT?

Taylor's career has seen her try so many different things, it's hard to predict what she'll achieve next! However, she clearly won't be slowing down any time soon. *1989 (Taylor's Version)* will be released in October 2023, coinciding with the final North American date of her ongoing Eras Tour. The shows are an epic career-spanning celebration with a theatrical set divided into ten acts, one dedicated to each of her albums. Taylor was clearly happy to be performing live again – "I can't even go into how much I've missed you," she told the audience on the tour's opening night.

Whether it's new albums, her next re-recordings, or more live performances, whatever Taylor does next, we're ready for it!

Taylor has teased the upcoming *1989 (Taylor's Version)* as being her favourite re-record so far: "The five From The Vault tracks are so insane. I can't believe they were ever left behind."

> **TAYLOR'S CAREER IS UNPARALLELED AND HER MUSIC AND INFLUENCE HAS RESONATED WITH MILLIONS OF PEOPLE ALL OVER THE WORLD.**
>
> THE BRITS STATEMENT ON THE PRESENTATION OF TAYLOR'S GLOBAL ICON AWARD

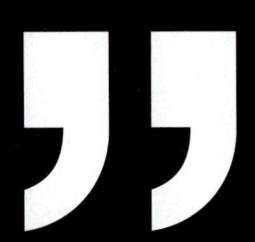

RIGHT: In May 2021, Taylor became the first ever female artist (and the first non-British person) to be honoured with the BRITs Global Icon award. Past recipients include David Bowie and Elton John.

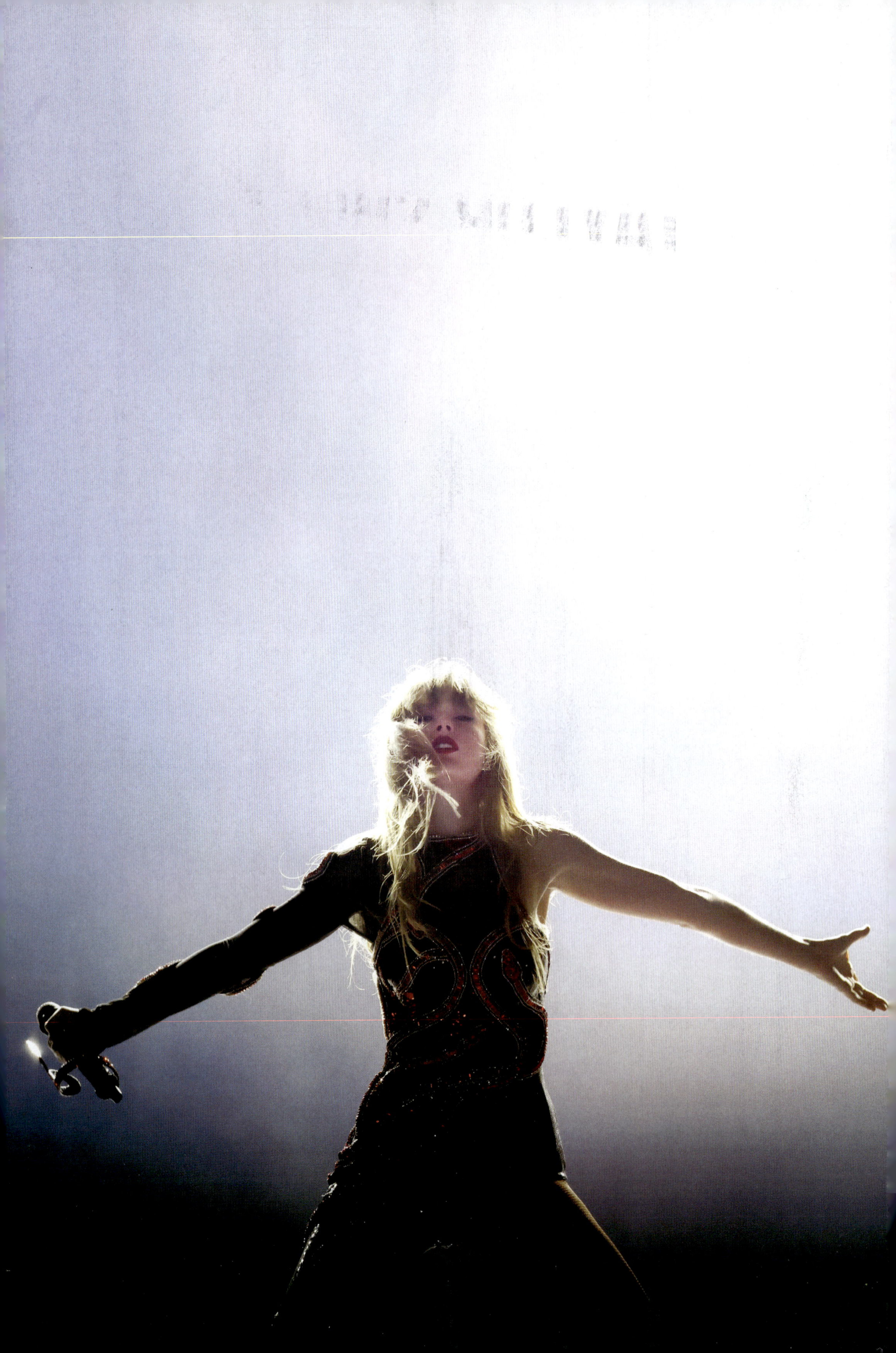